Play Matters
Investigative learning for preschool to Grade 2

Second edition

Kathy Walker

Published in 2025 by Amba Press, Melbourne, Australia
www.ambapress.com.au

First published in 2007
This edition was published in 2011 by ACER Press, an imprint of
Australian Council for Educational Research Ltd

© 2025 Kathy Walker

Photographs with thanks to Penbank School, Lauriston Girls School, Sholem Aleichem College and St Albans Primary School.

This book is copyright. All rights reserved. Except under the conditions described in the Copyright Act 1968 of Australia and subsequent amendments, and any exceptions permitted under the current statutory licence scheme administered by Copyright Agency Limited (www.copyright.com.au), no part of this publication may be reproduced, stored in a retrieval system, transmitted, broadcast or communicated in any form or by any means, optical, digital, electronic, mechanical, photocopying, recording or otherwise, without the written permission of the publisher.

Copying of the blackline master pages
The purchasing educational institution and its staff are permitted to make copies of the pages marked as blackline master pages, beyond their rights under the Act, provided that:
1. the number of copies does not exceed the number reasonably required by the educational institution to satisfy its teaching purposes;
2. copies are made only by reprographic means (photocopying), not by electronic/digital means, and not stored or transmitted;
3. copies are not sold or lent; and
4. every copy made clearly shows the footnote ('Copyright © Kathy Walker 2011').

For those pages not marked as blackline master pages the normal copying limits in the Act, as described above, apply.

Edited by Elisa Webb
Cover design by JAC Design

ISBN: 9781923569089 (pbk)
ISBN: 9781923569096 (ebk)

A catalogue record for this book is available from the National Library of Australia.

Contents

Preface	vi
Terminology	ix

Chapter 1 Early childhood education — 1

Introduction	2
Teaching and learning in the 21st century	3
Moving from preschool to primary school: A developmental perspective	4
Child development, personalised learning and intentional teaching	8
Defining the differences between curriculum, pedagogy, philosophy and values	9
Common misunderstandings	13
Summary	15

Chapter 2 Play-based pedagogy — 17

Introduction	18
Types of play	18
Stages of play	19
Children's thinking processes through play	21
Summary	23

Chapter 3 The Walker Learning Approach — 25

Introduction	26
Key principles	27
Core elements: The non-negotiables	28
The WLA for the preschool years	30
Summary	31

Chapter 4 Implementation — 33

Introduction	34
Successful implementation of a teaching and learning philosophy	34
Summary	43

Chapter 5 Setting up the learning environment — 45

Introduction	46
Classroom organisation and resources	46
Requirements of the indoor learning space	47
Requirements of the outdoor learning space	51
Literacy and numeracy	52
Summary	54

Chapter 6 A typical day using the Walker Learning Approach — 55

Introduction	56
Morning session	56
Instruction throughout the rest of the day	61
The teacher's role	62
Summary	63

Chapter 7 Planning and documentation — 65

Introduction	66
Principles of the planning process	66
Planning stages	67
Recording and documenting the learning	72
Summary	75

Chapter 8 Assessment and reporting — 77

Introduction	78
Benchmarks and standards	78
Assessment as opposed to testing	79
Assessment strategies	80
Reporting strategies	81
Summary	83

Chapter 9 Embedding child development, literacy and numeracy intentions 85

Introduction 86
Principles of literacy and numeracy within the WLA 86
Key organisational factors in establishing a rich WLA literacy and numeracy curriculum 90
The teacher's role 94
Summary 95

Chapter 10 Personalised and inclusive learning 97

Introduction 98
Children with special or additional needs 98
Ensuring all children can work effectively during investigation sessions 99
Children from diverse backgrounds, including Indigenous communities within Australia 101
Summary 103

Chapter 11 Informing and educating parents 105

Introduction 106
Suggested strategies and processes for parent information 106
Summary 109

Chapter 12 Frequently asked questions 111

Common concerns or misunderstandings of parents 113

Appendices 115

Developmental domains 116
Key WLA principles 117
Key procedures for implementing the WLA 118
Daily record sheet 119
Statement of intent 120
Individual record sheet 121
Relief teacher WLA information sheet 122
Parent helper information sheet 123

These appendices are also available as downloadable files.

References 125
Index 127

To Shona Bass for her insights and updates that have contributed to the second edition.

Preface

Many schools and children are now enjoying the Walker Learning Approach (WLA) in the early years of school. Since publication of the first edition of *Play Matters*, I have witnessed significant enhancement of oral language, behaviour, school attendance, engagement, literacy and numeracy in schools across the country that are using the approach. The approach is now in its 15th year of implementation and the data and results throughout this period have enabled me to enhance the continued implementation of the approach ensuring effective learning occurs.

The WLA engages children in exciting, personalised and authentic learning experiences that reflect the particular needs, interests and strengths of the individual child. It ensures a greater level of engagement for all students (particularly boys) and significantly reduces behavioural issues within the classroom. It also helps to increase oral language for all children regardless of their linguistic background, and integrate rich literacy and numeracy into all learning experiences (Walker 2009).

The WLA emphasises that learning is much broader and deeper than just literacy and numeracy and focuses parents, teachers and children on the 'whole' child. Ideally the WLA involves a total commitment from schools (or at least teams of teachers). It is not just about adding in a bit of play or more time for children to engage in some active learning. The WLA requires all the core elements being introduced, with whole-school understandings and leadership support. It includes both explicit daily instruction of literacy and numeracy alongside personalised learning opportunities in active engagement investigations.

There are some key elements of play as a teaching and learning tool, integral to this approach, that are explored in the chapters of this book. Each chapter provides information, ideas and instruction about the range of facets to the WLA across the years from preschool to Grade 2 in order to assist teachers, principals and teams to understand and implement the approach in a successful and sustained way.

Chapter 1: Early childhood education

This chapter identifies the key components required for effective teaching and learning in the 21st century for young children. It links the preschool and school years and discusses aspects of how understanding children's development, culture and life experiences impacts on the need for personalised learning. It also defines and discusses the terms curriculum, pedagogy, philosophy and values.

Chapter 2: Play-based pedagogy

This chapter provides an overview of play as pedagogy. It discusses the types of play, how it facilitates and links to learning and skill acquisition and how play is a mix of child initiated and teacher directed.

Chapter 3: The Walker Learning Approach

This chapter provides the overview of the WLA approach. It discusses the key principles and aspects of the approach that are considered 'not negotiable' and are required in order to provide effective teaching and learning. It includes ideas for modifying and adapting the approach for the preschool years.

Chapter 4: Implementation

This chapter provides the practical aspects required for effective and sustained implementation. This includes the importance of leadership support, whole team mentoring, whole school understanding and specific stages for implementation.

Chapter 5: Setting up the learning environment

The actual physical environment is an integral aspect of how the teaching and learning will work. This chapter provides the practical ideas and resources that are required in order to effectively set up the environment and to ensure rich literacy and numeracy experiences are also included.

Chapter 6: A typical day using the Walker Learning Approach

This chapter provides a comprehensive outline of the key features of a typical day using the WLA. It describes how and when literacy, numeracy and other subject areas are included and how the balance between investigation and formal instruction time occurs throughout the week. It unpacks the key aspects required for investigations including tuning in, reflection and focus children.

Chapter 7: Planning and documentation

This chapter highlights the importance of rigorous planning and documentation and provides examples of how the planning works each week and term and links to each state/territory framework.

Chapter 8: Assessment and reporting

This chapter provides details and examples of the range of observations, assessments and collation of samples of work that can be used to share with parents and students. It highlights the importance of students and parents being included in the assessment process.

Chapter 9: Embedding child development, literacy and numeracy intentions

Literacy and numeracy are still taught explicitly in discrete sessions throughout a week in a WLA classroom. This chapter provides examples of how literacy and numeracy are also embedded within the investigation sessions.

Chapter 10: Personalised and inclusive learning

This is a completely new chapter unique to this edition which provides examples and ideas for using the WLA with children with special needs and in Indigenous communities as well as for children from culturally and linguistically diverse backgrounds.

Chapter 11: Informing and educating parents

This chapter provides examples of how to work effectively and inclusively with parents to help them to understand and appreciate the teaching and learning within the WLA.

Chapter 12: Frequently asked questions

Over the years, a range of questions have been raised by teachers and parents about many aspects of the approach. This chapter provides responses to some of the most frequently asked questions.

This book provides the practical strategies that will assist teachers and school communities to implement the WLA with rigour, and provides information as to how the week can be balanced between active investigations and all the other literacy and numeracy we need to instruct children with.

I have noticed increased interest across the country in implementing WLA elements in the preschool years, before formal schooling begins. Obviously, explicit formalised instruction is not part of the preschool curriculum, but I encourage preschool teachers to use the elements that are appropriate for their groups.

I wish all teachers, and the children being taught, a wonderfully exciting time learning with the Walker Learning Approach.

Terminology

The specific approach being discussed in this book is referred to as the Walker Learning Approach (WLA). It is a personalised, investigative play-based pedagogy particularly in the early years context. The official title of the approach is the Australian Walker Learning Approach (WLA)™.

Across Australia, different terms are used to refer to grade levels in schools and to the year before school. In this book, we define preschool as the year before formal schooling commences, when children are in a play-based program and usually four or five years old.

Many terms are used in schools to describe parts of children's play. There are also approaches such as Reggio Emilia, Montessori and Steiner. The WLA, while reflecting some elements of play, is a unique and specific pedagogy. The approach is not about old-fashioned developmental play sessions, nor what is often referred to as language experience.

In this book, children's learning through concrete hands-on experiences is referred to as investigations. These descriptors are referred to as learning experiences rather than activities. It is important to use the language of investigations, work and learning when using the WLA, as children, teachers and parents need to understand that what might be known as 'play' in the general community is not the sort of play or investigations being used in the classroom.

Play is often viewed as the reward for when real work is complete. This is not how the term is used in the WLA. Play is part of the learning and work of children and integrates many aspects of literacy and numeracy.

Using the WLA and the associated terminology with children helps them to view their investigations as learning, and to understand that investigations and play are not a novelty or free time, but work time every day in the classroom.

Chapter 1: Early childhood education

'It is paradoxical that many educators and parents still differentiate between a time for learning and a time for play without seeing the vital connection between them.'

Leo F. Buscaglia

Introduction

The WLA is based on the concept of developmentally appropriate practices. Programs based on this theory have taken a variety of shapes and forms over the past five decades and primarily have an emphasis on acknowledging that both developmental and environmental influences impact on each individual's ability and timing of learning. The WLA has been designed from a perspective that reflects a range of cultural, demographic, economic and social factors. The program seeks to ensure that classrooms are filled with highly motivated children who are learning how to learn with a mix of active investigation and formalised instruction alongside opportunities for greater levels of decision-making, choice, active participation and a wide range of mediums in which to explore, learn and acquire skills.

As children move through the early childhood years (0–8 years), the transition from preschool into primary school requires teachers to ensure that many of the teaching and learning strategies children experienced as preschoolers are maintained and built upon. These eight years of maturation, growth and brain development require the young learner to not only have instruction in literacy and numeracy but also lots of concrete, hands-on, real materials and resources to interact and construct with. Alongside the recognition that children are more highly motivated to learn and sustain their own learning if they are engaged through opportunities to make authentic choices, ensuring a seamless transition between preschool and the first years of school was one of the original aims of the WLA.

The importance of consistent teaching and learning practices across a school community is only now becoming more apparent, accepted and acknowledged in mainstream schools. It is important for children and their families to be clear about the teaching and learning strategies and philosophies that are used across the school and that these strategies and philosophies are consistent, shared and constantly reflected upon. The old days of teachers being locked away in their individual classrooms should be well and truly over! The old comment, 'I just like to teach my own way, and it doesn't matter how the teacher next door teaches', is inappropriate. There is so much important research that highlights the need for clarity of philosophy and consistent practices right across a school (Livingston, McClain & DeSpain 1995; Weinstock, Starr & Fazzaro 1974).

We often make the comment that, 'It is not the child who must constantly adapt and change to different teaching methodologies, it is the teachers and the school community as a whole that are required to ensure consistency of philosophy and pedagogy'. Some teachers and even some leaders of schools are sometimes confused by this. They feel that each teacher has a right to do their own thing in their own way. They fail to understand or accept that as educators we must provide a consistent set of strategies, and that we now have access to a range of significant and highly valid research which can guide and support schools in developing their teaching and learning approaches (Summers 1994). Obviously each teacher maintains their own unique personality, and translates some of the practices and philosophy into their own manner. However, it is imperative that school communities provide consistent teaching and learning across the school which reflects and directly and consistently translates the school's educational philosophy.

The WLA provides a platform of evidence, research and practical strategies to schools which seek high levels of student engagement, motivation and personalised learning; and for students to be independent learners who are acquiring skills, not just 'content'.

The content of curriculum (literacy, numeracy, science, health, history, etc.) will always be found in government framework documents which change regularly. The WLA works in all states and territories and easily incorporates the wide range of content in each framework document, and the planning ensures that all requirements are met. The emphasis of the WLA, however, is not on the 'what' (curriculum) but most importantly the 'how' (pedagogy).

In this chapter we take the time to discuss the real and authentic elements of educating children in the 21st century, and developmentally appropriate practice for preschool to Grade 2 is explained more fully. Aspects of education that are needed to set children up to be successful learners, to know how to learn, to love learning, to be resilient, to problem-solve, to think laterally and to view life as an opportunity to learn no matter how old they may be are addressed. The often misunderstood terminology related to curriculum, pedagogy, values and philosophies is clarified. The chapter concludes with the contextual importance of leadership within the school and how that may influence the learning journey of the school community.

Teaching and learning in the 21st century

Children need to be provided with a solid foundation of skill acquisition and to develop a range of thinking and research abilities in order to learn how to learn. It is our responsibility as educators to ensure that children are provided with these learning opportunities. We cannot possibly teach the content or knowledge of all there is currently to know in the world, or predict what information will be necessary in the future. We can, however, provide learning environments that offer lots of practice in how to make decisions, initiate ideas, persist, find out, try again, take risks, explore and research in a range of ways that relate to children's own unique interests and endeavours; and to balance this with the areas of content and information that we as educators wish to introduce and provide.

> *Teaching and learning in the 21st century requires acknowledgement that successful education needs to provide a set of fundamental foundation skills that are transferable and adaptable for whatever the future holds.*

The results of research indicate that there are a number of key components required for successful learning to occur and to be sustained and transferable into the future (Time, Learning and Afterschool Task Force 2007). These include:

- intrinsic motivation

- relationship building and trust between students and staff

- empowerment and ownership of the learning

- engagement through authentic and relevant interests of children

- acquiring the skills of effective research, problem-solving, risk taking and resilience

- an emphasis on skills rather than knowledge or content

- learning how to learn

- a positive and realistic sense of self

- resilience

- working independently and interdependently.

The results of research also identify a number of factors conducive to student engagement (Bandura 1997):

- Students are more likely to engage and find learning meaningful if they have some ownership of their learning and the learning environment.

- Students require some opportunities for their learning to be personalised thus ensuring that the particular strengths, needs and interests of each student are best met.

- Students require opportunities to contribute to their learning, to make ideas and to offer suggestions that are factored in legitimately as part of the teaching and learning.

Most educators would agree with the points above, but there is vast diversity in the interpretation and application of these aspects of learning. For example, authentic and relevant interests require educators to personalise as many aspects of learning, projects and expectations as possible. Setting out a scope and sequence chart with predetermined topics years ahead of meeting the class of children (or before they even begin school) does not provide a personalised opportunity for students to become engaged in learning through their own authentic interests; it presumes that all students must somehow adapt their interests to fit the current topic. In the WLA, topics and predetermined units of inquiry are not necessary and cannot be taught in parallel with this approach.

The WLA's starting point is the authentic interests of the child alongside learning intentions from curriculum frameworks. By moving away from the starting point of a topic or unit of inquiry, the WLA immediately opens up a greater range of opportunities for students to have their own interests embedded within the areas of information and skills that schools are required to meet.

The WLA not only ensures that curriculum obligations for content and skills are maintained and enhanced but that this is achieved by teaching strategies that truly and effectively personalise, engage, empower and provide greater ownership and choice for students. It is after all, the students' learning that is most important, not educators' predetermined interests or topics.

The methodology of engagement, motivation, teaching and learning is the foundation the WLA is built upon. Through our work over the past 15 years we have collected data to ensure that not only are children motivated by and engaged with a range of authentic learning experiences but that literacy, numeracy, reading and writing are enhanced and sustained through this approach.

The WLA is an evidence-based pedagogy. Our own studies across years P–2, as well as data collected by schools for state and federal purposes indicate that children's oral language, attendance, punctuality, general eagerness and engagement with school and learning have all increased significantly under the WLA (Walker 2009). We have noted that while both boys and girls have higher levels of engagement in the WLA, it is particularly pleasing to see that young boys—who often display behavioural challenges—are strongly engaged and less prone to behavioural problems.

The philosophy and implementation of the WLA consistently demonstrate that engaging children is the first fundamental 'must' for successful teaching and learning. Underpinning this fundamental must is the understanding that compliance does not equate to engagement— engagement represents children being truly and authentically interested and excited in what they are doing and that it is real, relevant and meaningful to them as unique individuals.

The WLA seeks to ensure that engagement, motivation, consistency of practice and a shared philosophy across a school all work in the interests of students to maximise each individual child's opportunity to find the learning environment truly relevant, meaningful, exciting and successful.

Moving from preschool to primary school: A developmental perspective

Growth and development in children is characterised by sequential changes in their physical self, maturation, thinking, perception, skills and attitudes. These changes are also influenced heavily by their environment and the types of experiences children have been exposed to thus far in their lives.

Regardless of the stage of age and development, all children (and adults) learn most effectively when there is hands-on, real life exposure to learning opportunities that are as personalised as possible and relate in meaningful and engaging ways to each particular child and their interests.

Children develop best when they have secure, consistent relationships with responsive adults and opportunities for positive relationships with peers. Notably, positive teacher–child relationships promote children's learning and achievement, as well as social competence and emotional development.

Several prominent theories and bodies of research view cognitive development from the constructivist, interactive perspective (Naylor & Keogh 1999; Slavin 1990; Strike & Posner 1985). That is, young children construct their knowledge and understanding of the world in the course of their own experiences, as well as from teachers, family members, peers and older children, and from books and other media. They learn from the concrete (e.g., manipulatives); they also are capable of and interested in abstract ideas, to a far greater degree than was previously believed (Slavin 1990). Children take all this input and work out their own understandings and hypotheses about the world. They try these out through interactions with adults and other children, physical manipulation, play and their own thought processes—observing what happens, reflecting on their findings, imagining possibilities, asking questions and formulating answers. When children make knowledge their own in these ways, their understanding is deeper and they can better transfer and apply their learning in new contexts (Copple & Bredekamp 2009).

Play and active investigation are all important vehicles for developing self-regulation as well as for promoting language, cognition and social competence in children of all ages. Play gives children opportunities to develop physical competence and enjoyment of the outdoors, understand and make sense of their world, interact with others, express and control emotions, develop their symbolic and problem-solving abilities and practise emerging skills. Research shows strong links between play and foundational capacities such as memory, self-regulation, oral language abilities, social skills and success in school (Copple & Bredekamp 2009; Jones & Reynolds 1992).

Children's experiences shape their motivation and approaches to learning, such as persistence, initiative and flexibility; in turn, these dispositions and behaviours affect their learning and development. Development and learning advance when children are challenged to achieve at a level just beyond their current mastery, and also when they have many opportunities to practise newly acquired skills.

Promoting a seamless curriculum between early childhood and the early years of school is of major importance. Greater recognition of the unique stage of development in the early years, particularly in relation to brain research, has increased the interest of schools to implement further opportunities for children to engage in meaningful learning that is pitched realistically at their level (Newberger 1997).

What is developmentally appropriate practice?

Developmentally appropriate practice (DAP) has been associated with early childhood and early years education all over the Western world since the 1950s (Copple & Bredekamp 2009). In recent years, alongside a range of additional perspectives of early childhood, DAP has grown and reshaped to inform practices not only within the early childhood years but right throughout the primary years. Many aspects of DAP are used as the platform for the WLA.

DAP is a perspective within early childhood education whereby a teacher or child caregiver nurtures a child's social, emotional, physical and cognitive development by basing all practices and decisions on (1) theories of child development; (2) individually identified strengths and needs of each child uncovered through authentic assessment; and (3) the child's cultural background as defined by community, family history and family structure (Copple & Bredekamp 2009).

In the DAP environment, children are engaged in authentic, meaningful learning experiences through intentional teaching techniques, as well as by capitalising on teachable moments. Educators do not just teach to the whole group, but use a variety of grouping strategies, including small groups, pairs and 1:1 teaching. Personalisation becomes a key component in making sure the needs and interests of each child are focused on.

DAP is based on the idea that children learn best from doing: when they are actively involved in their environment and build knowledge based on their experiences rather than through passively receiving information. Active learning environments promote hands-on learning experiences and allow children to interact with objects in their environment, as well as their peers and teachers.

The concept of DAP requires an environment offering content, materials, activities and methodologies that are coordinated with a child's level of development and for which the individual child is ready. Children's development follows individual patterns and timing; children also vary in temperament, personality and aptitudes, as well as in what they learn in their family and within the social and cultural contexts that shape their experiences. Three dimensions of appropriateness must be considered:

- age appropriateness
- individual appropriateness
- appropriateness for the cultural and social context of the child.

The temporal pattern of children's development and learning is characterised by varying rates from child to child, as well as uneven rates across different areas of a child's individual functioning. Individual variation is subject to the:

- inevitable variability around the typical or normative course of development
- uniqueness of each child as an individual.

All children have their own strengths, needs and interests. The enormous variation in development among children of the same chronological age highlights that a child's age is only a crude index of developmental abilities and interests. For children who have special learning needs or abilities, additional efforts and resources may be necessary to optimise their development and learning. The same is true when children's prior experiences do not give them the knowledge and skills they need to thrive in a specific learning environment.

Given this normal range of variation, decisions about curriculum, teaching and interactions with children should be as individualised as possible. Rigid expectations of group norms do not reflect what is known about real differences in development and learning. At the same time, having high (but realistic) expectations for all children is essential, as is using the strategies and providing the resources necessary to help them meet these expectations. Development within a DAP framework proceeds toward greater complexity, self-regulation and symbolic or representational capacities.

Pedagogical best practice aligned with developmentally appropriate practice

The WLA philosophy recognises that the children's learning environment and development are not only influenced by biological factors, but also through the influences and experiences they are exposed to in their home environments. This book highlights the reality that the way young children learn, and the teaching and learning strategies that are required for this learning, are unique to the early years of school and distinct from those of older children and adults.

From the beginning of school to Grade 2, sound pedagogy requires that children have active, concrete, hands-on experiences every day that are balanced and linked to formal instruction (i.e., in the middle of the pedagogical continuum). The question however, is not where on this continuum the pedagogy needs to be, but rather how to reliably and consistently achieve this without the pedagogy becoming free play and didactic teaching.

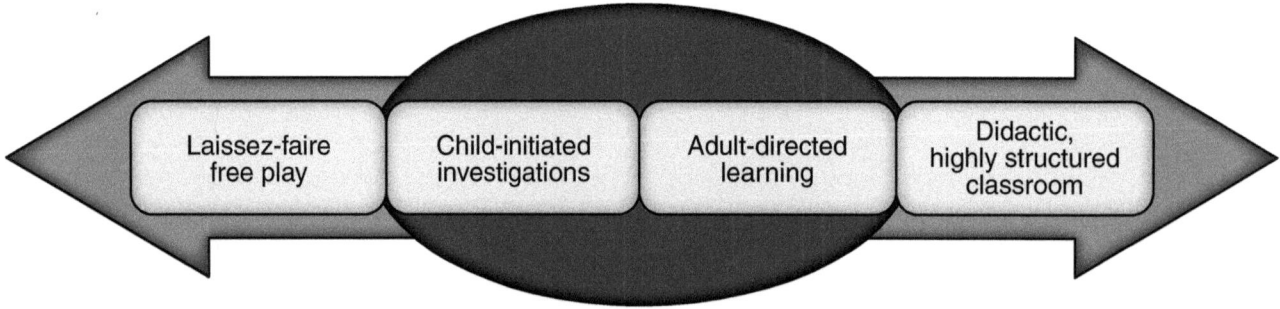

Figure 1.1 Pedagogical continuum. Young children must have a mix of both teacher instruction and concrete hands-on experiences, not one at the expense of the other.

Adapted from Miller, E & Almon, J 2009, *Crisis in the kindergarten*, Alliance for Childhood, College Park, Maryland.

As educators, we are challenged to ensure that the early childhood learning environment:

- recognises this unique stage of the lifespan by providing appropriate experiences

- engages children in relevant and meaningful learning to which they can relate

- engages both boys and girls and recognises and accommodates some of the differences between boys and girls in their development and approaches to learning

- provides hands-on, creative and concrete experiences

- provides a seamless approach to curriculum and teaching and learning strategies as children make the transition from their early childhood program into their first years of school

- provides experiences that link and interconnect literacy and numeracy with other learning so that young children find these skills exciting, fun and relevant to their lives

- recognises the social and emotional development of the child, as well as their development in the disciplines of literacy and numeracy

- reflects the individual needs, interests and experiences of children as they enter the learning environment

- promotes an exciting and stimulating learning environment that allows children to explore, investigate and further some of their own interests.

Consistent with these points, DAP includes the following teaching strategies:

Active learning experiences

DAP programs promote children's active exploration of the environment. Children manipulate real objects and learn through hands-on, direct experiences. The pedagogy provides opportunities for children to explore, reflect, interact and communicate with other children and adults. Learning centres are one means of providing active learning experiences; these are established in a defined area of the classroom, and promote a range of skills and experiences for learning and engagement, for example, the dramatic play area. Excursions, real life experiences such as cooking, re-enacting historical events, conducting scientific experiments and participating in community service projects are other examples.

Varied instructional strategies

DAP encourages the use of varied instructional strategies to meet the learning needs of children. Such approaches may include process writing, skill instruction, guided reading, modelled writing, cooperative learning, independent learning activities, peer coaching and tutoring, teacher-led instruction, thematic instruction, projects, learning centres, problem-based learning and literature-based instruction (American Association of School Administrators 1992; Privett 1996; Stone 2001). Providing a wide variety of ways to learn allows children with various learning styles to develop their capabilities, to view learning in new ways and also helps cater for multiple intelligences.

Balance between teacher-directed and child-directed activities

DAP encourages a mixture of teacher-directed and child-directed activities. Teacher-directed learning involves the teacher as a facilitator who models learning strategies and gives guided instruction. Child-directed learning allows the child to assume some responsibility for learning goals.

DAP informs the differentiation of teaching approaches for children's evolving stages of development. As children develop, the pedagogy of play develops to deepen the children's processes and engagement. Figure 1.2 demonstrates this differentiation from preschool to lower primary and upper primary years. In the preschool setting, the focus is on play-based curriculum with intentional and responsive teaching, 1:1 or 1:small group with no formalised instruction. The lower years of primary school require concrete, hands-on, investigation-based experiences balanced with intentional teaching; that is 1:1, 1:small group and formal instruction. In the middle and upper years

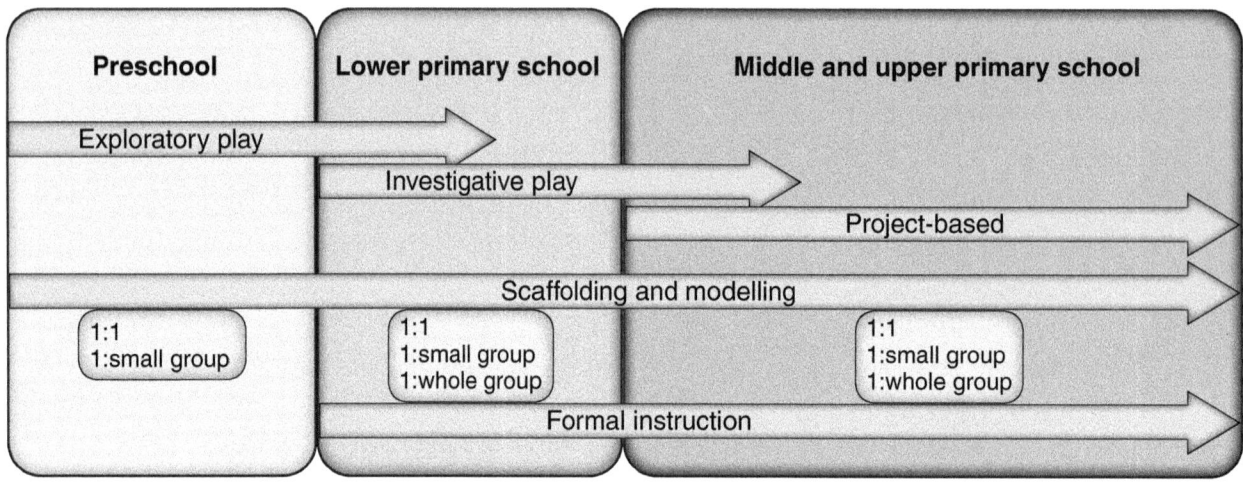

Figure 1.2 Developmentally appropriate practice informs the differentiation of teaching approaches that are appropriate for children's stage of development

of primary school, hands-on investigation takes the shape of projects with intentional teaching 1:1, 1:small group and formal instruction.

Child development, personalised learning and intentional teaching

The WLA places a major emphasis on the maturity and development of each child. Identifying the developmental maturity of each child and setting objectives for class groups around their development helps to focus the teacher on the realities of the children in the group, and provides a framework for expectations that relate directly to the children's maturity.

Developmental domains

The developmental domains, as described below, are not the same as values. This is a particularly important point as there is often confusion between a value and an aspect of maturity. For example, we may have the value of cooperation, however, given children are developmentally mostly in an egocentric cognitive state in their early years of school, they are more likely to be interacting in parallel rather than cooperatively.

Developmental domains

- *emotional or affective*
- *social*
- *cognitive*
- *language*
- *physical*

See the CD appendix for an extended list of developmental domain indicators.

Factors related to development

- Development occurs generally in an orderly sequence although some elements of individual, family and cultural experiences also impact on learning.

- Development proceeds in predictable directions of greater complexity, organisation and internalisation.

- Children are active learners, drawing on direct physical and social experiences.
- Play is the most important vehicle for children's emotional, social and cognitive development.

Defining the differences between curriculum, pedagogy, philosophy and values

The WLA is a philosophy of teaching and learning that spans from preschool through to the lower, middle and upper primary years. It is not a curriculum or a teaching tool that is overlaid on an existing pedagogy, nor is it to be viewed as an 'add-on' program that needs to be squeezed into the existing overcrowded timetable. The WLA is a pedagogy that underpins everything that happens in a day, a week and a year—and informs every moment of the teacher's intention to teach (planning, scaffolding, modelling, observing and directing). The philosophy and pedagogy of the WLA from preschool to Grade 6 is based on student empowerment, engagement and ownership alongside teacher direction, scaffolding and instruction.

As an educator and researcher, I believe it is vital for schools to have clarity in key aspects of curriculum and philosophy to ensure that whatever major elements of teaching and learning are adopted within a school, there is consistency and transparency for teachers, parents and children. Schools wishing to implement the WLA require a clear understanding of what adopting a particular philosophy with associated teaching and learning strategies actually involves.

The terms pedagogy, philosophy, curriculum, program and values are often merged, used interchangeably, completely misrepresented or misunderstood. The table below provides a simple explanation of each of the terms to help school leaders and teachers clarify and purposefully plan their own school philosophy and pedagogy.

The importance of a whole-school philosophy

The exploration of any teaching and learning approach (and its subsequent implementation) requires school communities to clearly articulate the philosophy and practices to parents, teachers, children and others. Nothing can be more confusing and challenging for a school community than the fragmentation of practices and/or inconsistencies in approaches. Teachers, parents and children can become quite confused and lack confidence in what the school actually believes in if messages are inconsistent or unclear because there is no purposeful platform of philosophical understanding.

The more consistent and clearly articulated the overall philosophy and practices are within a school, the more effectively they can be introduced, supported and sustained. The results of many studies from across the world highlight the effectiveness and quality of teaching and learning when a consistent set of principles and practices are shared, understood and implemented rather than when individual teachers implement their own interpretations of curriculum requirements (Summers 1994; Weinstock, Starr & Fazzaro 1974; Wright, Horn & Sanders 1997). Many schools across Australia are now spending more time on internal professional development and meetings to work through what type of educational philosophy and associated pedagogy needs to be reflected across the whole school. At times this can be a challenging process. Some teachers may be resistant to change. Others may feel threatened or that the way they are teaching is being criticised.

In some education communities, the concept of an education philosophy is not well understood; this introduces complicating factors when trying to develop and embed a whole-school philosophy. For example,

- schools often have a mission or vision statement and a three-year strategic plan which are touted as the school's 'educational philosophy'
- terminology such as, 'to value individuals', 'to help every child succeed' or 'to build strong literacy and numeracy' are often mistakenly

Examples of developmental practice using the Walker Learning Approach

- The physical environment is not dominated by tables as the major focus of the room. Contained, defined spaces for children are established.

- The environment provides defined spaces and individual learning spaces as well as opportunities to work alongside each other.

- To a considerable degree, children are able to self-regulate, self-select and act independently within the learning environment without having to have all materials, resources and equipment provided by the teacher.

- Individual records and observation are taken of the children both in relation to learning objectives and their development.

- Opportunities for individual interests are provided by the teacher.

- Children's development and learning is viewed as the main starting point for planning learning objectives.

- Children's culture, family and individual strengths and needs are built into the range of experiences provided.

- Inclusive language and diversity are promoted through the integration of books, language used by staff and the resources provided.

- The use of outdoor space is provided as a legitimate learning area.

- Active hands-on learning through investigations and play is the major tool for teaching and learning.

- Explicit instruction is most often provided in small groups, but whole-group instruction, meetings and discussion are still used.

- Time is provided for children to engage in their learning so that they can complete tasks and gain a sense of achievement.

- Creative and open-ended experiences are some of the major strategies used for teaching instruction.

- A variety of learning centres, including dramatic play, construction, collage, writing and sensory areas through play are provided each day.

- Time for physical and quiet experiences is embedded throughout the day.

- Reflection of children's own learning is integrated into each day.

- Children have opportunities to continue an area of interest into a project or ongoing contact work.

- Some of the learning is planned with children, and opportunities are given to children for self-assessment.

- Intrinsic motivation is a key aspect of the WLA. Extrinsic rewards, stickers and stars are not used.

- Assessment is based on observation, samples of work, portfolios and individual records.

- Parents and children are involved in reporting and interviews for discussion together.

- Parents are encouraged to participate in the learning with their children.

- The teacher scaffolds, responds to and directs children through their learning experiences.

- Mixed ability groupings may be used but are not necessary.

Table 1.1 Terms and definitions to help leadership and teachers clarify and purposefully plan their own school philosophy and pedagogy

Term	Definition
Educational philosophy	A set of key beliefs based upon specific theoretical perspectives, research and values that underlie all practices in teaching and learning. An educational philosophy is not a framework designed by state or federal governments. A philosophy helps individual schools interpret and respond to government requirements and informs how teaching and learning will look.
Pedagogy	The 'how' of all teaching, learning, interactions and strategies which reflect and relate directly to the philosophy and are used consistently across a community.
Curriculum	Technically, curriculum refers to everything contained within an educational setting: the content, teaching, relationships, resources, environment and the 'how'. It is an overarching term. It is often mistakenly interpreted only as the content, outcomes or as a syllabus.
Program	This is a specific (often stand-alone) training unit such as a resiliency program, a restorative justice session or a social skills program.
Values	The underlying beliefs that a school places as a thread or context on which all teaching, learning and modelling are reflected. A value technically cannot be taught, but must be embedded within a school community.
Framework	Most frameworks provide an overview, outline or list of teaching and learning skills, knowledge and understandings that a state or federal government requires of schools. It rarely reflects a philosophy or pedagogy; most often it is a list of outcomes.
Outcomes/objectives	In recent years, education circles have adopted the term 'outcome' from economics. It refers to particular skills or knowledge that it is anticipated students will reach at particular times, years or grade levels. Outcomes can only be called outcomes once a student has achieved something. What are often labelled as 'outcomes' at the planning and framework stage should in fact be objectives, goals or intentions.
Tools	These are particular teaching activities that teachers use to help and support themselves and students in the teaching and learning process. Tools such as De Bono's thinking hats or Gardner's multiple intelligences for example are not educational philosophies or pedagogies; they are tools that can be used within particular philosophies, including the WLA.

used as a philosophy. These statements are values that may be embedded within the philosophy but are not actually an educational philosophy that guides the practice of all staff working within that school

- teaching and learning tools are mistakenly used and thought of as an actual philosophy with associated key principles and practices. De Bono's six thinking hats is not a philosophy or pedagogy, nor is multiple intelligences. These are simply a range of interpretations of other theories that have been translated into particular tools for teaching alongside key principles of practice. Many schools which use the WLA would incorporate aspects of thinking hats or multiple intelligences simply as one part of a great whole in teaching and learning strategies.

Developing a whole-school philosophy

An educational philosophy is developed by following these well-defined and purposeful steps and processes:

1. Identify the key values the school community believes to be most relevant.

2. Match these values with theoretical underpinning.

3. Identify research that indicates the most effective teaching and learning strategies.

4. Identify educational philosophies and practices that best match the values of the school and the research that has highlighted best practice teaching and learning.

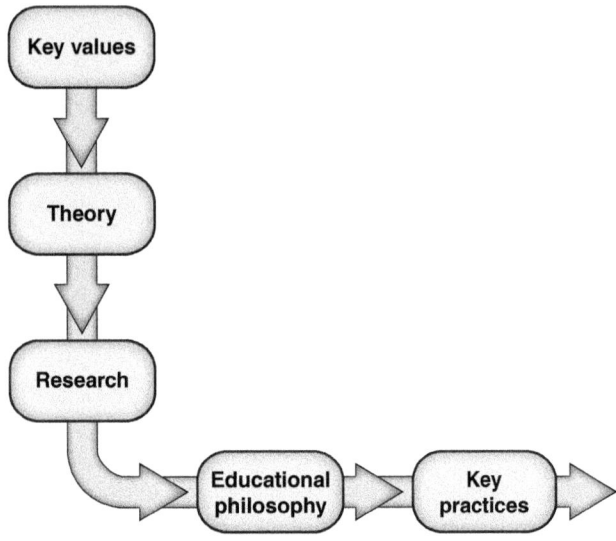

Figure 1.3 Process for the development of educational philosophy and practice

Note: Curriculum framework expectations are simply integrated within the existing philosophy and pedagogy.

An actual educational philosophy that has teaching strategies to match is an imperative for long-term effective teaching and learning within a school community. It is not appropriate or conducive for effective teaching and learning for each individual teacher or teaching team to implement their own style based simply on their past experiences or preferences. Few professions would accept separate practices within one professional community. This does not mean that all teachers are clones of each other and that there is no room for individualising learning environments that reflect the nature of the teacher and the students.

> *There is a significant difference between (i) a teacher just doing their own thing in their own room divorced of any deeply considered philosophy and research in education and (ii) a teacher making their own interpretation of the clarity set out in the school's philosophy.*

Most schools that reflect strong leadership and commitment to a particular philosophy will also implement strategies to ensure the consistency of pedagogy continues even when leadership or staff move out of the school. This is demonstrated when schools advertise for staff that are aware of the key philosophy, principles and practices embedded within the school and have the skills and understanding to embrace this philosophy in their classrooms. Another example is when interview panels and questions are specifically determined to identify potential staff members who have an understanding of the particular philosophy and pedagogy of the school.

Strong and effective leadership will result in the core philosophy of the school being perpetuated even if there is a change in leadership. If a new principal is appointed in a school, the philosophy and pedagogy should not be changed overnight—this indicates that the appointment has been based on criteria which are not congruent with the most significant aspects of the school; that is the philosophy. A major factor of any appointment should be that the new principal embraces, understands and is committed to the philosophy of the school. This is one of the great challenges in mainstream education today. How does a school develop, sustain and implement a clear and consistent philosophy and pedagogy, and how is it maintained through staff and principal selection?

An educational philosophy directly informs how the teaching and learning will occur throughout the school community. Ideally, when implementing an educational philosophy such as the WLA, leadership and the school community have taken time to explore, understand, test and learn about the philosophy. The adoption of the approach, therefore, becomes an informed and well-understood process that provides support to staff and information to parents and the wider community. This ensures not only successful implementation of the philosophy and successful learning for students, but a sustained and ongoing commitment to the philosophy that attracts likeminded teachers into the school. It also ensures leadership that has clarity and conviction of how the teaching and learning needs to look across the school or team.

> *Not all children are ready to learn the same thing, at the same time, in the same way. Not all children will be ready to meet the same benchmark or literacy level at the same time, as environmental and developmental influences impact on children's rate of learning.*

Common misunderstandings

Sometimes the WLA is misrepresented or misunderstood. It can be mistakenly assumed to have no direction, planning or goals. It is often confused with terms such as 'developmental play' or 'free play' time. In reality, the WLA is a major pedagogical tool that teachers use throughout the day, integrating opportunities for children's interests and investigations to link directly to elements of literacy and numeracy and other areas of learning. All teaching should be intentional, including the planning, the provocations, the language of learning, the scaffolding and the formal teaching.

In addition to intentional teaching, child-centred pedagogy must be responsive to the individual child. All teaching is explicit whether the teacher is scaffolding, modelling or directing. The WLA pedagogy is intentional and responsive both during investigations (child-initiated and adult-directed) and formal teaching (instructional and adult-directed). The WLA seeks to use elements of children's interests alongside practical, hands-on learning experiences that quickly engage children in the learning process. Teaching uses the explicit interests of the children plus new ideas from teachers in instructional times to help motivate and engage the children.

The WLA uses key elements of children's development, learning and the social environment in which they live and experience life. It seeks to scaffold children's learning through making explicit links and opportunities for children to find their learning. It also allows for the acquisition of useful and sustainable skills over time.

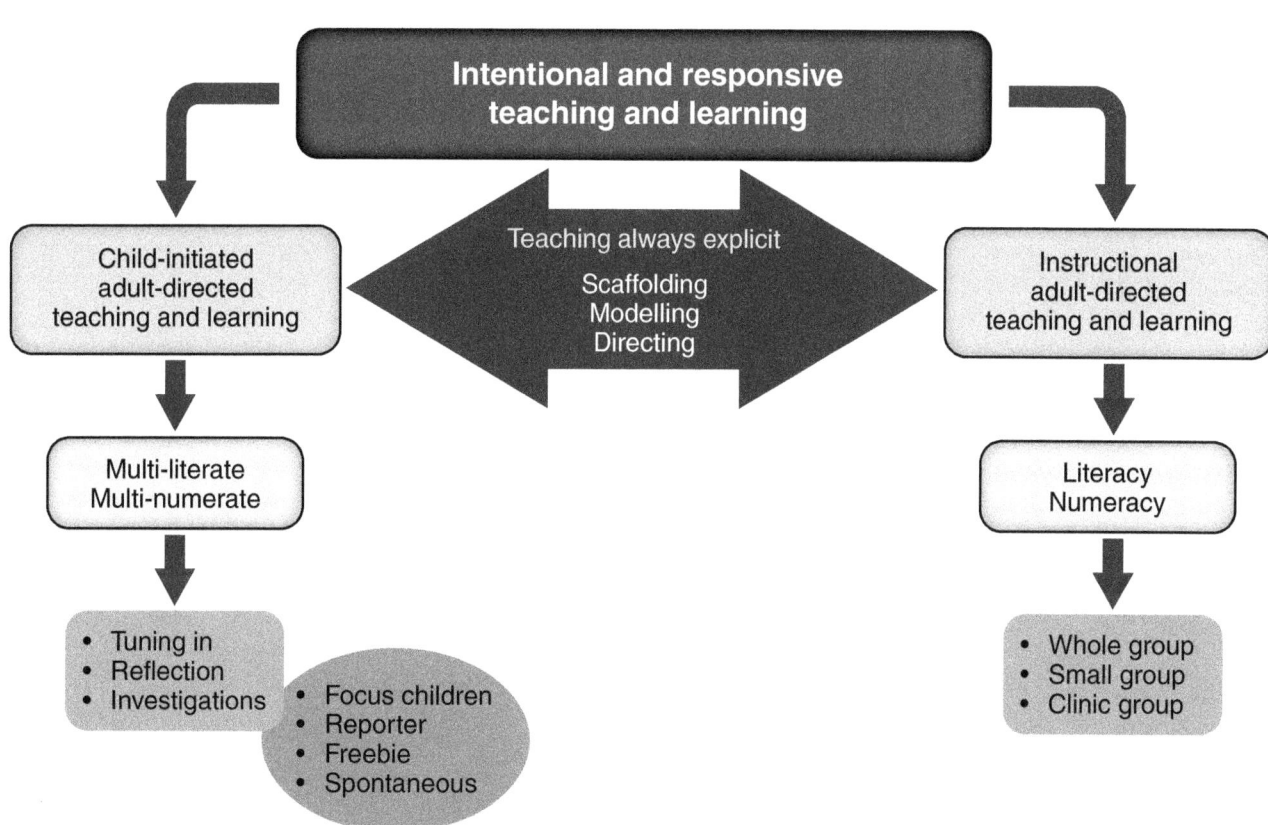

Figure 1.4 Intentional and responsive teaching and learning

Some key aspects of the WLA are:

- creativity and open-ended tasks are encouraged over cloned artwork; for example, limited or no use of worksheets that all have the same stencilled outline

- promoting knowledge, understandings and skills through the hands-on constructions, creations and dramatic play in which children are engaged

- children's interests are an integral part of planning, in contrast to scope and sequence charts with topics or units of inquiry that are predetermined by teachers

- intentions for learning and development are the starting point for planning

- that it seeks to ensure that not only girls, but also boys are actively engaged in their learning and that boys are not set up to experience frustrations associated with some of the specific aspects of boys' development.

Embracing the challenge

Education itself is at an interesting time in history. As educators, we know more than we have ever known about children's development, learning styles, personalities, the link between learning and family input, brain research and general development of children. We have seen a range of innovative strategies being introduced to learning environments over the years. Yet we are faced with the tensions and challenges of a society that currently uses the language of benchmarks, outcomes, standards and testing and is far too closely linked to accountability at a bureaucratic level than to what we actually know about children's development and learning.

The WLA philosophy places the child (and the reality of children's development at this early stage of life) at the centre of curriculum planning and expectations. It is opposed to attempting to fit children into preconceived levels or preset outcomes that they are not developmentally ready to attain. Intentions and expectations for their learning are still planned for and worked toward, but a predetermined outcome is not set.

Goals and intentions are still identified and worked towards. Expectations for children's learning are still set. However, the rate of acquisition, the way in which learning is achieved and the range of strategies for teaching within the WLA are the key issues that this book considers, and for which it provides guidance and practical strategies.

The WLA in the early years of school can be an exciting and dynamic approach that places the child at the centre of the curriculum and provides a rich range of personalised learning opportunities that are truly reflective of the child's age, stage and interests. It can provide a learning environment that is an invitation to children to explore, investigate, experiment and discover that learning is fun, productive and achievable.

Summary

- The WLA is based on developmentally appropriate practice.

- The WLA promotes a seamless curriculum between early childhood and the early years of school.

- Effective teaching and learning ideally requires a strong commitment to a shared philosophy and pedagogy that is consistent across a school.

- Teaching and learning must emphasise skills and 'learning how to learn', and not be preoccupied only with content and knowledge.

- Students require empowerment, ownership, engagement and motivation as key criteria with which to learn and sustain learning and skills.

- Students require a mix of active investigation, research and some freedom to explore and construct learning based on their own interests alongside guidance, scaffolding, direction and instruction from their teachers.

Chapter 2

Play-based pedagogy

'We want to give our children everything – but inadvertently they benefit less because we give them everything.'

Shona Bass

Introduction

Implementation of the WLA requires an understanding and knowledge from leadership and teaching teams of play as a learning tool. The medium of play as a learning tool for children has been examined and researched for many decades. Despite a general view of children and their play as frivolous, fun or undirected, many theorists over the years have presented successful theories and perspectives on play, and there is a rich history of using play as a learning tool. Play theorists include:

- Friedrich Froebel (1782–1852)
- John Dewey (1859–1952)
- Margaret McMillan (1860–1931)
- Rudolf Steiner (1861–1925)
- Maria Montessori (1869–1952)
- Susan Sutherland Isaacs (1885–1948)
- Lev Vygotsky (1896–1934)
- Jean Piaget (1896–1980).

While each theorist and perspective reflects a range of different interpretations and emphases on children's learning and play, there are some fundamental points about the nature of play and children's learning that are useful for teachers when exploring teaching and learning strategies within a play based approach:

Play activities involve a wide range of behaviours and can be situated in different contexts, which may have multiple meanings for children ... Play can be regarded as deeply serious and purposeful ... It can be characterized by high levels of motivation, creativity and learning ... (Wood & Attfield 2005, p. 2)

There are many different forms of play and investigations. The WLA provides a broad range of experiences and types of play so that children are immersed in a rich range of thinking, oral language, literacy and numeracy experiences alongside opportunities to consolidate their social and emotional maturity.

Types of play

Imaginative and socio-dramatic play

Children use a range of materials in fantasy, in creating and representing their own ideas and understandings through imaginative play. In acting out, imagining and representing through play, their thinking and oral language skills are enhanced. This is one of the major ways in which children construct, make sense of and understand their world.

Constructive and investigative play

Children require hands-on, concrete materials such as Lego, Mobilo, blocks, collage and interest tables in which they can construct, design and create a range of representations from their own imaginations.

Explorative play

This is the type of play where children are investigating the properties of things; finding out, exploring the environment, trying things out, often with mediums such as water, magnets, sand and magnifying glasses.

Directed and scaffolded play

This is where children are encouraged or prompted in their investigations by an adult or a peer. It may be that the teacher requires a particular skill or exploration to be undertaken and so the child is directed or supported in this.

Sensory play

This is a very important part of children's learning. They require sensory experiences through things such as water, clay, finger paint, scent, aroma and touch. This is often an area that is neglected in the learning environment and it helps particularly with children's emotions, to be calm and to have a safe outlet.

Investigations and play must be viewed as the main vehicle for learning to occur. Play is the child's work and is not viewed by the child as a novelty.

Stages of play

Onlooker play

We are often concerned if we observe a child who is watching others and not joining in with their work or interactions. This can be a legitimate stage of a child's development. They are watching, taking information in but not quite ready to engage or enter the play themselves. Even as adults, we at times take a step back to observe others.

Solitary play

This is the stage where children will work alone and attempt to keep themselves slightly removed from others. They engage in their own world of play and investigation and are neither aware nor interested in others at this time.

Parallel play

Children work alongside others, are aware of the play and interactions of others but predominantly are still working at their own project or investigation. They may at times speak or interact minimally with others, but this is most often if they are interrupted by someone else or require one of the resources being used by another child. This stage is quite frequent and evident in children as they move from preschool to school.

Associative play

This stage reflects maturing cognitive development. Children are slightly less egocentric and are much more aware of others. They may work together on similar projects at times and can take particular roles in their play and work. However, it is not as mature or refined as the next stage (cooperative). This stage is often confused with cooperative interaction and work.

Cooperative play

This is a very mature aspect of cognition. It occurs mostly in children moving into Grades 2 or 3. It requires some degree of empathic understanding and a wider range of perceptions of others' feelings and needs. It is not a type of interaction that we would aim for in the early years of school although opportunities through play will reflect some children moving into that stage.

In the early years, children will often work individually in solitary play, and at other times, in parallel and associative play. A key feature of the WLA is that it encourages and allows children to work on their own and in association with others. It does not expect or force children to work cooperatively together.

> *One of the teacher's roles is to provide a rich range of opportunities for children to explore, investigate, involve and engage in purposeful, personalised and meaningful experiences, so that a number of different types of play, thinking, reasoning and understanding can occur.*

Play used as a teaching and learning tool is not 'free play'. We do not just allow children to play when the real work is finished, or employ play to help children settle in. Play is always purposeful, linked to learning objectives and is the major strategy for teaching and learning. This is a key point in this approach.

Some key characteristics of play

Child-initiated play

Child-initiated play does not mean the adult cannot suggest, prompt, guide or scaffold in particular directions. However, at some stage, in some way, the child is able to engage in a purposeful investigation that is of authentic interest to them. As Kelly-Byrne writes, 'The dramatic play of children is an alluring and incredibly complex kind of behaviour that is likely to encompass most, if not all, of a child's resources and integrate them into a whole' (1989, p. 212).

Symbolic play

This usually involves some element of pretend, imagination or role play. Through the investigation of a range of materials or equipment provided for the children, each child may create or reflect a particular role, medium, product or project that is representative to them of something in real life.

Play as a process not just an end product

The investigation, creation, or work of a child may not necessarily always have to result in an end product. The process itself may be providing the practice of skills, thinking, creating, imagining or simply engaging in an experience that is purposeful and meaningful to the child at the time.

It is not necessary for every child's investigations to be completed, nor does the child's engagement in their investigation need to be sustained over a period of a day or a week.

Play is active and creative and avoids worksheets and cloned expectation

Play involves the child actively engaged in an exploration which is purposeful and investigative. It will involve some element of creativity and provides the opportunity for the child to demonstrate their own ideas, understandings or needs. Play should not reflect an approach where each child has to make the same cloned egg or daffodil or clock. It is the child's mind, the child's skill and the child's learning, not the teacher's.

Play involves children creating experiences that reflect their own interests. Colouring in pre-drawn stencilled shapes are not part of the WLA.

Play is owned by the child not the adult

The play or experience belongs to the child. The adult may scaffold, intervene, extend, make suggestions or provide a direction. However, the child views the play or project as his or hers.

Play reflects the interests of children

A major aspect of the WLA approach is that the play reflects both the interests of the child and adult. Adults watch, observe, listen and talk with the children in order to ascertain what interests, ideas and directions the children can be encouraged to pursue as part of the learning process. This is sometimes known as the emergent curriculum—watching to see what ideas the children reflect or respond to and then scaffolding the learning and skills from those interests (Stacey 2009).

Play is purposeful

The play and learning of the child involves them in a purpose, constructive exploration or investigation that may be planned for, reflected on and linked for the child to their learning and interests.

Play involves literacy and numeracy

Literacy and numeracy are embedded within most life experiences. While discrete instruction through clinic groups or whole group instruction will still occur, the WLA approach recognises the richness and breadth of literacy and numeracy through the range of children's play and investigations. Teachers utilise these experiences to link explicitly back to literacy and numeracy understandings and skills.

Play promotes social skills

Through engaging in investigative play-based learning experiences, children will sometimes work independently and at times in association with others. Through role-play, acting out, problem-solving, dealing with conflicts, trying out different tasks, negotiating, turn-taking, speaking and listening to each other, the WLA approach provides a rich range of social opportunities that are authentic and embedded within the natural way of interacting. There is less need to provide specific and separate social skills instruction, as this occurs naturally through play.

Play promotes oral language

Oral language is a critical element of the early years of learning. The most effective means to promote oral language is to provide a rich range of opportunities for children to engage with each other, to experiment and practise with words, language and conversation.

In dramatic play, social interactions, solving problems together and reflecting together at the end of each session on their play and learning, oral language is significantly enhanced. Oral language is also developed when children have the opportunity to engage in repeat conversations about the same things with adults (Copple & Bredekamp 2009). The development of oral language underpins all aspects of learning and is the major contributor to a child's comprehension.

Viewing play as a learning tool

Play is in itself a learning tool and children come to view this approach as part of their learning. For children, active engagement and investigation is considered to be a normal and integral part of the work that takes place during the school day.

Play in the learning environment must:

- be well-planned and directed by the teacher
- involve the adult in observation and scaffolding
- occur inside and outside
- promote creative opportunities
- link with literacy and numeracy
- include the arts, society and community
- include assessment, observation and reporting
- be integrated into the day as a major part of the learning and not as a separate time that has no relationship or link to any other learning
- not be seen as the novelty or prize for good behaviour or finished work.

Children's thinking processes through play

A number of key aspects of thinking and lifelong learning skills are facilitated through children actively engaged in learning through play. Some of these skills include:

- a range of thinking skills
    - reasoning
    - perspective taking
    - problem solving
    - lateral thinking
    - divergent thinking
- oral language
- mathematical understandings and experiences
- literacy
- self-regulation and self-expression
- intrinsic motivation
- skill acquisition and practice
- self-initiation and decision-making
- responsibility
- questioning
- reflecting
- resilience.

Neurological studies

In recent years, a number of key studies have highlighted that in order for early brain development to occur productively, children's brains require stimulation (Mares, Newman & Warren 2011). The nature of this stimulation includes two major elements:

1. Human attachment—meaningful relationships and consistent interactions with other children.

2. A rich, stimulating environment that promotes creativity, active investigation and concrete, real experiences relevant to a child's stage of maturation and life experience.

This brain research is reassuring for the classroom teacher when implementing investigative play into the learning environment. Providing children with time to engage meaningfully in their investigations and to be actively involved in their own projects, is providing the stimulation the brain requires in these early years.

Links between learning, teaching and play

Play provides the most natural and meaningful means by which children can construct knowledge and understandings, practise skills, immerse themselves naturally in a broad range of literacy and numeracy and engage in productive and intrinsically motivated learning environments. The children's interests provide great 'leaping off' points for teachers who can use these interests to introduce skills and understandings.

International research confirms that classroom teaching and learning tools must be relevant and appropriate to the child's stage of maturity in order to sustain learning in meaningful ways, to promote an intrinsic approach to children's learning as well as to help children see that learning is not separate from life, but is an integral part of life (Lindsey 1998). Studies suggest that creative, open and active learning environments produce happier children, less behavioural disruption in the classroom and significantly engaged children who learn productively, sustain their learning over the long term and can transfer the skills they acquire to a range of different learning situations (Copple & Bredekamp 2009; Marcon 2003).

Summary

- Within play, there are many subsets or different types of play and learning that are occurring.

- Play is the most effective means for providing rich, diverse thinking and oral language, social skills, and problem solving.

- Children's play reflects different levels of maturity.

- Play as a pedagogy must be planned for, directed by and facilitated by the teacher.

- Play is viewed as part of the learning process rather than an add-on program.

- Play has been researched for many decades in relation to the significance it holds in children's lives including for social, emotional, psychological and intellectual development and learning.

- Play is a natural way of children exploring their environment and learning about themselves and their world.

- Many skills are acquired through children's active exploration and investigation of their world.

Chapter 3
The Walker Learning Approach

'It is becoming increasingly clear through research on the brain as well as in other areas of study, that childhood needs play. Play acts as a forward feed mechanism into courageous, creative, rigorous thinking in adulthood.'

Tina Bruce

Introduction

The WLA is an evidence-based pedagogy—that is, the original design was informed from theoretical understandings of child development, child behaviour and child psychology which underpinned the theory of best practice in pedagogy for early childhood. This theoretical design was then developed according to what is realistic and what really works at the coalface—in the classroom, the school and with teachers, children and parents. The approach was tested by independent researchers over a period of five years using an 'action research model'—data was collected every few months and the results from each data collection were used to develop the approach further. Over this time, the model became deeper, richer and more successful at engaging children in real, relevant and meaningful learning.

Figure 3.1 Evidence-based pedagogy

Although the approach has evolved and developed over time, the major aims remain consistent. They include:

- **To build a bridge between the preschool years and the early years of school.** In other words, to ensure a smooth transition as children move from preschool to school, with a seamless curriculum and continuity of teaching and learning. I always think how strange and disappointing it is to have children move from a rich and highly engaging play-based curriculum in preschool and then only five-and-a-half weeks later, enter a classroom that has nothing but chairs and tables and sometimes no opportunity to investigate at all.

- **For all children, particularly boys, to engage deeply and meaningfully with their learning environment.** I want all children to find learning exciting and related to some of their own interests and to be engaged with a rich range of experiences to investigate, explore and create with.

- **For children to learn that the skills of literacy and numeracy are meaningful and useful parts of everyday life.** While these skills are still taught explicitly in sessions throughout a week, the WLA aims to embed multi-literate and multi-numerate experiences in children's lives through their investigations (for instance, counting how much money they need for the shop, dialling phone numbers from the home corner, speaking in front of the group about their learning, reading texts and writing experiences throughout a day), rather than developing a mindset that literacy and numeracy are skills to be learned in isolation.

- **For children to have more authentic opportunities to learn social skills, conflict resolution, problem-solving, decision-making and independence.** I want us to stop talking at children so much about these concepts and instead provide them with daily opportunities to live and experience them as they interact with others during investigation time.

- **For children to enjoy school.** Not just to learn to be compliant, behave and do what they are told, but to engage deeply, to develop an authentic sense of themselves as learners and to view learning as relevant to their own lives and experiences.

- **For children to have opportunities that reflect their own culture as well as to have exposure to new concepts and experiences.**

- **To move away from pre-planned sequences of predetermined topics**. These often do not reflect culturally relevant or engaging experiences for children and tend to perpetuate a belief that all children have to be engaged in the same topic for the same length of time.

- **For children to have more authentic and frequent opportunities to have their learning personalised and to build skills of personal reflection, intention and evaluation early in the school life**.

The WLA promotes personalised learning and reflects that in their early years of school, young children require the mix of explicit instruction alongside active, hands-on investigations. This chapter explores the key principles of the WLA (which are also included on the CD), as well as the core elements of the approach—the 'non-negotiables'.

Key principles

The WLA is a rigorous approach in education requiring teachers to recognise, plan for and implement a range of strategies that clearly identify learning and development objectives.

The WLA philosophy and pedagogy are underpinned by high quality, highly powered research (Miller & Almon 2009) that demonstrates comprehensively that from the beginning of school to Grade 2, children require active, concrete hands-on experiences that are balanced and linked to formal instruction (see Figure 1.1 on p. 6).

As stated in Chapter 1, the question is not where on this continuum the pedagogy needs to be, but rather how this can be achieved reliably and consistently without the pedagogy becoming unconnected sessions of free play or didactic teaching (ends of the continuum).

When the core elements of the WLA are implemented with integrity and rigour, the children will be engaged in their learning, it will be developmentally appropriate, it will be authentically personalised and it will be in the middle of the pedagogical continuum.

As vital and important as literacy and numeracy are, learning is so much more than just those two things. It is about finding yourself, your interests and skills, and developing and embracing a love for learning for all of life. The early years are the most wonderful time in which to actively investigate and learn.

The WLA is based on a sound set of theories and perspectives on children's development and learning, and attempts to reflect what is known as the 'whole' child. Learning is about the academic but it is also about the social, emotional and cultural influences (Copple & Bredekamp 2009; Hirsh-Pasek, Golinkoff, Berk & Singer 2008). The key principles underpinning the WLA are:

- Childhood is a unique stage of the human life cycle and children, particularly in their early childhood years (birth to eight years), reflect unique biological characteristics that have implications in how they learn.

- Each child has his/her own rate of development and influences from home and society that impact on learning.

- Not all children will be able to learn the same thing at the same time in the same way.

- Development, while generally sequential, varies between children of the same chronological age.

- Family, community and society are integral to children's understandings and learning.

- Not all children will be interested, or able to engage in the same topic or interest, and thus the learning environment must reflect to a large degree, opportunities for children to learn through their own interests as well as some introduced by the teacher.

- Learning is more meaningful when experiences reflect children's lives and are presented in ways that reflect the child's stage of development.

- Learning involves not only skills and understandings but is heavily influenced by elements of development within the five developmental domains (see Chapter 1).

- Development in one domain influences, and is influenced by, development in other domains.

The WLA is an entire approach and philosophy, not simply one pedagogical tool or system. This means that rather than just adding one particular additional tool, the approach is holistic and impacts on everything within the learning environment.

The WLA reflects the fact that nothing magical or mysterious occurs inside a child's brain or learning style over the end-of-year holiday period as they leave their early childhood program behind and commence the next step in their school learning.

The child who left the early childhood program is the same child who enters the school classroom six weeks later: the same child who needs to learn in the same way as they did during their early childhood years.

Core elements: The 'non-negotiables'

The core elements of the WLA are those elements that have been proven by 15 years of active research to be critical to the integrity and success of the approach; this is why they are considered 'non-negotiable'.

Each school and teaching team will have their own culture, personalities, strengths and challenges. However, while these differences will remain between schools, any school that is implementing the WLA should have the core elements in place. Specific details of how the days and weeks work in the WLA are unpacked in Chapter 6.

Investigations

At least four mornings each week, the day will start with active, hands-on experiences for the children known as investigations. Each day there will be formal instruction in numeracy, literacy and specialist subjects. The experiences of the children and the explicit teaching that takes place during investigations are used as a springboard into the formal teaching of the day. These experiences will have been planned intentionally by the teacher, building on the emergent (children's interests) and core (school/community interests) curriculum.

Every day of investigations will involve three focus children, a reporter and a photographer. Each investigation will begin and end with the teacher scaffolding and modelling the children. These 20-minute sessions are referred to as 'tuning in' and 'reflection' respectively. The actual hands-on active engagement (investigating) requires a minimum of 45 minutes.

Tuning in and reflection

Intentional rigorous planning is required for the teacher to successfully and effectively scaffold and model during tuning in and reflection; the planning process and how the planner is used to inform all components of investigation is explained in Chapter 7.

Tuning in is for the learning for the whole day and includes four key parts:

- welcome and administration
- reflection and revision of literacy and numeracy intentions
- focus children, reporter and photographer scaffolding in front of group
- intentional direction at dispersal.

During investigation time, the teacher:

- works individually with focus children, reporter and photographer
- scaffolds children who need support and/or extension.

Reflection time is the 'springboard' into formal teaching and includes four key parts:

- scaffolding focus children, reporter and photographer

- the teacher modelling particular skills and concepts from investigations

- freebies (children who are chosen to demonstrate a specific skill)

- setting up and packing away ready for the rest of learning.

Focus children

The idea is that each child will be a focus child for the whole day once a fortnight in an average term of 10–12 weeks. A roster system is organised with all of the children listed over a fortnight so that parents, children and teachers know who will be a focus each day.

Focus children have some key roles:

- They stand at the front of the group for a few minutes during tuning in time so that the teacher can scaffold and discuss in front of the group what they may be working on during investigations. Children may ask questions or offer suggestions to the focus child.

- The teacher honours the authentic interests of the focus child and uses these interests as the platform to scaffold and model the learning.

- During investigations, focus children spend a few minutes each on their own with the teacher. This ensures relationship building, personalised scaffolding and time for the teacher to get to know more about the child.

- Focus children report back at reflection time on their learning. Children ask questions and the teacher highlights specific examples of learning, skills, behaviour and values that are worth drawing attention to.

Reporter and photographer

The reporter and photographer are teacher-directed roles. The teacher introduces the task and requirements of the reporter and photographer at tuning in each morning in front of the other children. Children are encouraged to offer suggestions. At reflection time, the reporter and photographer report back and share whatever their task was. Children are then encouraged to make comments, ask questions and make further suggestions.

The purpose of the reporter is for the child to:

- look on, talk with, listen and respond to other children through the investigation time and to 'report' back some of what they observe the children making, learning or investigating

- use a pen and paper on a clipboard in the first instance to help document what they observe or to report back on what they have been asked to find out during investigation time.

The reporter's task is set by the teacher. In this way, each child has a personalised task set for them. The reporter role is a favourite role as each child feels special and has a task that scaffolds their learning without being too difficult or demanding. The reporter only has to carry out the role for part of the investigation time and then they can proceed back to their own investigation.

As children move into Grades 1 and 2, the reporter's tasks can be more skill-based and link to any aspect of learning that the teacher thinks is appropriate. For example, a reporter might do some data collecting, put it into a pie graph and have it ready to upload and show at reflection time. They might have to take notes at certain timed intervals on particular children's work. They may have to observe and unpack what skills or learning they thought certain children were reflecting.

The photographer role is similar to the reporter's. The task is set by the teacher and may involve a broad range of skills and tasks. For example:

- time sequences of different investigations being undertaken

- before and after photos

- examples of particular skills being demonstrated

Early in the year, the photographer's role could be as simple as photographing the focus children or finding as many different shapes as possible around the classroom.

The WLA for the preschool years

Developmentally appropriate practice, by definition, ensures that whatever grade a child is in, the teaching and learning can accommodate itself to meet the capabilities and needs of that child.

The WLA system established for children once they commence school—with a morning tuning in, focus children, reporters and photographers with reflection time toward the end of a session—is slightly modified for the younger cohort.

It is up to the individual preschool teacher as to how much and when they use the tuning in and reflection system such as in the actual model used for school-aged children, but there are some key points that are relevant and can be used as a guide for implementing the approach in the preschool program.

- Greater use of small and informal groups is used in the preschool years.

- A morning tuning in may be appropriate, but would be shorter than 20 minutes and early in a year would provide general discussion about the learning and experiences of the day rather than formalising the focus children or reporter roles.

- Focus children can still be used; teachers would still target these during the play sessions and still attempt to work individually with them over a fortnight to three weeks depending upon the size of the group. They would not necessarily be tuned-in in front of the group, but as the year progresses the teacher may implement this either in whole or small group sessions.

- As the year progresses, tuning in and reflection with focus children and reporters may be introduced depending on the group and individual children. It is not desirable to put the approach's system before the needs of the children. Some children may be tuned in while others continue to work at various centres around the room.

- Depending upon the children in the group, it is anticipated that during Term 3 or 4, many children would be ready for the tuning in, reflection, focus children and reporter/photographer role to commence. This will assist with a smooth transition into the first year of school.

- Planning based on both teacher intentions and what emerges from the children works in parallel, so the fortnightly statement of intent can be used. The elements of literacy and numeracy would be less formal and integrated within the play-based investigations.

- Learning centres are all based upon the same principles as for the first three years of school: open-ended, creative and providing a rich range of skills and explorations.

- The sessions would provide an informal snack time, allowing children to continue on with their work rather than having to pack away at the same time.

- Preschoolers would have an investigation journal or portfolio to capture photographs, samples of experiences and learning and these would be shared and jointly owned by the child, the teacher and the parent. They would be accessible to parents and children during sessions for perusal and discussion.

- Teachers would use the range of documentation as used by school teachers, including the daily/weekly record sheet, the individual child record sheet and the statement of intent. These would work alongside the state/territory/national framework outcomes and expectations.

Generally, all preschool programs offer a play-based curriculum that utilises a rich range of recording, planning, implementing strategies and programming systems. Within the WLA, it is suggested that the play-based curriculum continues and that the specific roles and aspects of the WLA for the first three years of school can be used, adjusted and modified depending upon the group and each individual child.

Summary

- The WLA recognises the unique developmental and biological maturation of children during the childhood years.

- Active investigations are used as the basis for the major teaching and learning tools that best suit young children.

- Play as a teaching tool is well researched and is proven to provide rich learning for children.

- The WLA is not an add-on or something that needs to be squeezed into an already crowded curriculum. The approach is the major way for teaching and learning to occur.

- Literacy and numeracy are embedded within the play—this develops multi-numerate and multi-literate opportunities.

- Discrete clinic and instruction groups are still used in both small and whole-group instruction.

- The interests of the children and their investigations are used as the basis for further instruction, skills and understandings.

- Topics are not needed and are never used.

- Integrated curriculum that uses a particular topic focus is not needed and cannot be implemented alongside the WLA.

- Planning stems from learning intentions in key learning areas and from indicators of development through the five developmental domains.

Chapter 4
Implementation

'The beginning is the most important part of the work.'

Plato

Introduction

Through my experience over the past 17 years, I have witnessed a whole spectrum of effective and sustained implementations of the WLA. In this chapter I present a synthesis of international research identifying the key elements of a successful execution of any new pedagogy, along with my own experiences working with leadership teams and teachers as they embrace the WLA philosophy to teaching and learning. Especially important are the processes that help professionals transition through change in the workplace.

Chapter 3 has described and unpacked how the WLA works in P–2 and the key elements contained within the approach. In this chapter I want to encourage the reader to carefully consider and understand the importance of the following suggestions and recommendations to avoid as many challenges and difficulties as possible. This will provide the opportunity for the school to enjoy the process of exploring and implementing the approach as well as to ensure that the integrity, quality and rigour of the approach are upheld. A summary of implementation recommendations is located on the CD.

We strongly recommend the following elements are considered when a school community wishes to embark on implementing the Walker Learning Approach.

Successful implementation of a teaching and learning philosophy

Leadership is everything

It may sound like stating the obvious, but leadership in education (particularly in education communities such as schools) is one of the most important, influential and empowering roles. Without strong, clear and visionary leadership, a school community almost always eventually lacks clarity of vision and philosophy and as a result lacks consistent practices.

Leadership is different from management. Leadership of an education community sets clear goals and looks to the future as well as considering the current perspective. Along with other key members of the school, the leader identifies the direction; philosophy and pedagogy of the community (see Figure 4.1).

It is often commented on—and I would agree—that the leaders within a school community best able to implement a whole-school philosophy such as the WLA are those who have expertise with and an understanding of philosophy and pedagogy. The importance of these qualities is

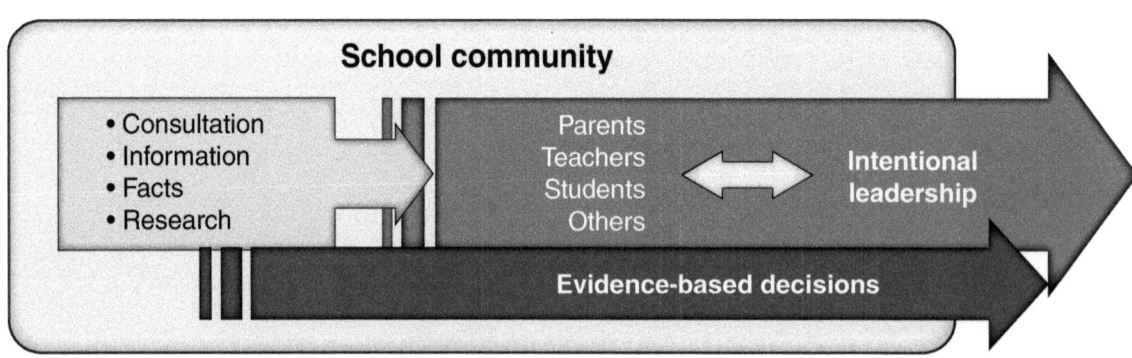

Figure 4.1 Process for intentional leadership for an education community

often underestimated, resulting in other staff with a lesser understanding of pedagogy, whole school philosophy and research about teaching and learning being assigned roles that are outside the scope of their expertise (for example, curriculum coordinators or professional development coordinators). Often a whole school approach is not even on the radar, rather professional development budgets are provided to individuals or teams that may all be doing things completely separately, in ignorance of and often in opposition to each other!

Recommendations for leadership

Some of the most effective implementations of pedagogical philosophies we have witnessed in schools which adopt and use the WLA, have happened when the principal and leadership team ensure the following:

- They have a full knowledge and understanding of the approach.

- In dialogue with teaching staff, they set the agenda and future direction of teaching and learning in the school.

- They ensure that parents and the entire school community are aware of and have some understanding of the direction and commitment of the school's teaching and learning.

- They allocate time, funding and resources in order to support staff throughout the implementation of the approach.

- They meet regularly with staff and attend the majority of staff professional development sessions, ensuring that they are aware of and understand the various stages, challenges and needs of staff.

- They provide information to other staff and support the implementation process so that the teaching team is not placed under any undue scrutiny or criticism from other staff during the initial implementation stages.

- They do not hedge their bets—that is, they do not sit on the fence claiming that a school can operate successfully with more than one philosophy.

Effective and ongoing evaluation and assessment of the approach in relation to teaching and learning should be built into the process. This is usually through an action research model that uses not only data from testing, but focus group discussions with students, parents and teachers along with anecdotal observations, longitudinal collection of additional skills such as social skills, motivation and engagement.

We recommend leaders avoid…

- a culture that endorses the mindset that each teacher can just teach the way they prefer

- allowing individual teachers to make decisions about the future direction of a school's philosophy and pedagogy. Teachers who find change difficult may take this as an open invitation to resist and will often obstruct an entire school or team from effectively being able to implement the approach

- trying to reach a consensus among an entire school community about the direction for the teaching and learning. Leadership actually needs (after due and respectful dialogue and discussion with others) to make a decision and set the direction

- trying to have bits and pieces of lots of different pedagogies. This is a recipe for disaster. It gives confusing and mixed messages to parents, teachers and students and does not provide a seamless or consistent set of teaching and learning strategies across a school community.

Fact finding: Clarity rather than assumptions

Many hundreds of staff attend professional development programs to find out about the WLA. This is part of fact finding, staff discussion and information gathering. It is interesting to note here that at the conclusion of a session, staff often make the comment, 'I wish my principal had been here, they don't understand about this at all.' We always recommend that the principal or someone from leadership attends an information session in the early fact finding period. Leadership attendance ensures that all staff, particularly those with decision-making abilities, are aware of and have received the same information. In addition, we often meet with the leadership team at the school, to ensure they know about the approach and what we recommend as a series of strategies for effective implementation.

Fact finding is an important part of making sure that any approach a school is thinking of putting into practice is well researched, based on sound theory, practical to implement and consistent with state, territory or national framework requirements. With any approach, there are people who think they may know or have heard about it, or claim to have tried it, without ever reading a book, reviewing the research or being provided with support, mentoring and professional development. This can be a dangerous situation; misunderstandings and a lack of knowledge about the approach can lead to inappropriate and poorly constructed practices, which in turn are ineffective in the teaching and learning process. Not only is this undesirable for the children, it also can increase the likelihood of giving the approach a negative reputation, despite the fact that the staff weren't actually using the approach as it was intended.

While we always encourage teachers to add their own particular skills and tools to the WLA, we do not endorse teachers changing and altering the approach to the point where the key elements (i.e. the non negotiables) that have been researched for over a decade cease to exist. This undermines the integrity and rigour of the approach. An educational philosophy and pedagogy is a science, and in the case of the WLA it has taken many years to develop, trial, research and review the approach to ensure that teaching and learning is enhanced rather than compromised. The WLA is far more complex than many teachers assume and ensuring that leadership and staff are aware of the how, what and why of it all, is a critical part of the early days before implementation.

Our key point here is to ensure that you find out the facts and work toward shared understandings across the school or team, which will help to avoid myths, misinterpretations and/or ignorance.

Creating an implementation plan

Once the fact-finding has been completed and the leadership and staff have made a commitment to implement the approach, we recommend a number of key strategies during the process. It is important to recognise that implementing an actual pedagogy as opposed to a discrete program requires forward planning, time and support.

In this process, Stages 1 and 2 are the most important; these recommended processes are considered to be the ideal preparation and support for successful implementation of the WLA. Stages 3 and 4 are additional options for schools/staff wishing to proceed further.

Stage 1

- All team members who will be implementing the approach: (i) attend an information symposium, (ii) visit a school with accredited teachers implementing the approach and/or (iii) attend a two-day study tour (descriptions of these professional development sessions are below).

- Leadership attends a symposium or an introductory overview session as a leadership team.

- At least 6 months lead-in time of preparation allowed before actual implementation.

- A whole-school overview of the WLA is conducted at a staff meeting after school or during a professional development session.

- A parent information session conducted by WLA staff is provided for further input and information sharing with the wider community.

Stage 2

- Mentoring—with a WLA accredited mentor who has implemented the approach in their own classroom as a teacher—commences.

- Mentoring provides assistance and information on planning, linking to literacy and numeracy, ensuring curriculum framework outcomes are met, learning environment set-up, resourcing, modelling tuning in and reflection and room set-up.

- Mentoring consists of a mix of discussions as well as model teaching in the classroom, observations and debriefs.

- Two mentor sessions are recommended for the teaching team in the term before implementation.

- Three mentor sessions per term are recommended for the first year and two or three sessions in the second year. (For rural, remote and regional schools these are usually conducted in either whole day, half-day or three-hour sessions combined with distance education support.)

- Regular updates with leadership team.

- A visit to other schools for observation.

- Sustaining the approach if there are changes in the teaching team or leadership.

- Attend a further study tour once 12 months into implementation.

Stage 3

- Moving the approach into other areas of the school.

- Accrediting staff who are successfully implementing the WLA.

Stage 4

- Being identified as a school to host visitors to model the WLA.

- Contributing to workshops and conferences.

Timelines

The anticipated timeline for full, successful implementation of the WLA in at least one whole teaching team, or whole school (depending on the amount of mentoring and professional development as well as the size of the team or school) is usually 12–18 months. Most change theories remind us that effective and sustained change requires time, reflection, evaluation and a period of adjustment (Marion 2002; Mazzuno 2001).

Study tours and professional development sessions

Providing teachers with professional development sessions ensures that all staff share an understanding of the theory and approach. Topics for professional development might include:

- introduction and overview of WLA
- child development theory and research
- implications of child development
- developmental domains
- types of play
- the role of specialist teachers
- planning approaches
- linking literacy and numeracy into play and projects
- linking explicit literacy and numeracy teaching to children's investigations
- integrating the curriculum
- assessment and reporting
- working with parents.

The WLA provides a range of different professional development opportunities to support, strengthen and sustain effective teaching and learning not only in the early stages of implementation but into the future (see Table 4.1).

Preparation and lead time

We recommend that schools or teams spend at least one term (preferably two) in lead time before

Table 4.1 Professional development opportunities and the WLA

Type of professional development	Description of professional development
School visits	Schools implementing the WLA throughout Australia, which provide opportunities for teachers to observe the learning environment and talk with teaching and leadership staff. We recommend visiting schools where the teachers are accredited in the WLA. Visitors are able to talk with the teachers and gain further insights into the approach. Most schools host visitors on days of symposiums.
Study tours (1 or 2 days)	These offer a practical and theoretical immersion in the approach, including professional development sessions alongside visits to at least three schools in either metropolitan or rural areas with a range of different socioeconomic and cultural demographics.
Symposiums	Symposiums of either half or full days conducted in all states and territories as either introductory or extension information and professional development sessions.
Whole/half day professional development	Sessions designed to meet the specific needs of the school or network. Sessions are developed from a mix of theoretical, practical and reflective practice and individuated scaffolding.
Whole school overview	Presented to the leadership and teaching team, including coaches and special educators.
Mentoring	With a WLA accredited mentor who has implemented the approach in their own classroom as a teacher. This is a combination of mentoring during and outside class time. Teachers are provided with instruction, model teaching, demonstrations, reflective practice and a scaffolding review. Remote, regional and rural teachers are offered the opportunity for mentoring using a distance education model.
Tele/Skype/video conference mentoring	Useful for any school but particularly for rural, regional and remote schools which are implementing the WLA but are not able to access regular mentoring and professional development due to distance.
Weekend conferences (1 or 2 days)	Generally conducted by organisations or networks of schools—usually a combination of keynote lectures and breakout sessions of practical application including videos of implementation in the classroom.
Group school mentoring	Offered as an additional service to support schools. Group school mentoring provides professional development in one location for teachers from different schools. It is not a replacement for individual school mentoring but does provide some further options for schools seeking to ensure effective and sustained implementation of the WLA. These group sessions are intended to be supplementary and complementary to individual school mentoring.
Parent information sessions	Conducted in the afternoon or evening to help parents understand what effective teaching and learning in the 21st century looks like and how the WLA operates in the classroom.

commencement. So many aspects of the approach require discussion, time and preparation. Gathering of resources, understanding the new planning formats, ensuring these link back to state/territory and national frameworks, commencing mentoring, visiting and observing schools and setting up the learning environment are all required to be organised before the WLA can be successfully implemented.

Principles of the WLA that can be translated into existing classroom practices

The WLA requires one to two terms of teacher and school preparation before implementation can begin in the classroom. During this time teachers can begin to move the learning environment closer to the WLA even before the more in-depth elements of the approach have been explored or undertaken. Keep in mind that all the core elements of the WLA must be implemented for the pedagogy to maintain its integrity; thus we urge teachers to avoid just using some of the strategies and attempting to fit them alongside or on top of everything else that is happening. This cannot be sustained and as discussed in this chapter, the WLA is a philosophy and a pedagogy that informs all aspects of teaching and learning in the classroom.

Creative, open-ended, non-cloned experiences

- Don't use worksheets and don't expect that all children will complete the same task. For example, instead of giving every child a paper plate clock with stuck-on hands on which to write the numbers, provide a range of art, craft and collage materials (including boxes, fabric, cardboard, paper, etc.) so they can construct and represent their own understanding of time.

- Avoid all children having to make the same object. For example, children don't need to all make daffodils in spring or snowmen in winter. The WLA aims to highlight children's own ideas and does not need themes or topics.

Promoting intrinsic rather than extrinsic motivation

- Children don't need stickers or stamps as a reward for work attempted or completed. The WLA prefers adult conversation, encouragement and opportunities for children to reflect and assess their own feelings about completed or attempted work.

- Avoid 'student of the week' awards. Children become quite used to these rewards and sometimes they are not truly authentic. There are many ways in daily interactions to recognise something special or significant without having a pattern that children and parents expect.

Providing opportunities for children to explore, investigate and create

- Instead of using a block of time for literacy, try to incorporate more open-ended tasks for children. Add in a dramatic play area such as a shop or post office that can link to oral language and literacy experiences.

Children need time to engage, to move away and to return to experiences

- Instead of packing away children's learning or experiences, try leaving this until after morning recess or lunch if possible. Provide longer periods of time for children to enter into the learning, to wander off and then to return to their work.

- If you are going to use some of your time for investigations ensure children have at least 1.5–2 hours, so they have time to engage and do not find it a rushed and unsettled experience.

Children need opportunities to reflect on their learning with others

- Starting the day with a short discussion about some of the investigations or play the children are planning or the teacher is directing them to, helps to frame the ideas for children.

- Have small groups or 3–4 children from the whole group reflect and describe their projects or play at the end of the session. This gives the teacher opportunities to model, scaffold or use some of their ideas for future explicit teaching.

A preschool child had made a 'specials' board in the dramatic play area of the classroom which had become a pizza shop. The child had written the 'S' in 'Specials' around the wrong way. This was a good opportunity for the teacher to model the letter and sound of 's' even though this wasn't actually planned.

Children have short concentration spans when sitting together in a large group

- Attempt to limit whole group times to 10–15 minutes at a time, or provide some choices for the children so they don't all have to attend all group times, but can continue with their projects or work.

- Experiment with different ways of conducting show and tell or do away with show and tell. Often this is a time when children disengage and don't really listen to each other. There are many other ways for listening and speaking to occur, and in the WLA, children have opportunities to do this for much of every day.

Children like defined and contained spaces to work and play in

- Try separating and/or taking away some of the tables.

- Individual mats for each table or masking tape in the shape of circles or squares helps to define the spaces for individual children.

- Use noticeboards or shelves to break up the room so that the tables are not all together in the centre of the room.

Children need learning to occur inside and outside the classroom

- If you have easy access to a wet area or extra space right outside the classroom, try to set up some painting easels, blocks or Lego in these areas.

Mentoring

Through any change process and the acquisition of new information and skills, support from experienced staff is important. Mentoring provides ongoing support to teams and schools implementing the WLA.

WLA mentoring is provided by WLA accredited mentors in a range of ways depending on the location, needs and timeline of staff:

- at individual schools in meetings and discussion with teams

- in the classroom (model teaching)

- via Skype and video conferencing/ teleconferencing

- group school mentoring (where staff from a few schools are mentored together).

Aspects of mentoring sessions include:

- planning

- environment set-up

- resourcing

- practical ideas

- links to literacy and numeracy

- how to conduct various aspects of the WLA including investigations.

- timetabling a week

- developmental domains

- links and auditing against state/territory and national framework expectations

- assessment

- documentation

- reporting

- model teaching of tuning in and reflection.

Parent information

Parents are an integral part of the school community. They not only help to shape policy and directions of a school in many cases, they are key partners in the learning processes of their children. They must be informed about the teaching and learning strategies being implemented within the school. Parents often expect to see learning look exactly like it did when they were in primary school. They can become confused, fearful or apprehensive if they see or hear about things that appear 'different' from what they believe school and learning should be. We find a series of strategies helps significantly to empower and inform parents and to help them feel at ease with some of the changes they may witness. These strategies are detailed in Chapter 11; the following is a brief overview:

- A parent information session conducted by our organisation that helps to set the scene for parents about what teaching and learning needs to look like and provide for young learners moving into their futures. An emphasis is placed on the facts that as educators we still instruct, explicitly teach literacy and numeracy, set limits and expectations, work within state/territory and national frameworks and in addition provide greater opportunities for children to develop skills that are imperative for success in learning and life (for example, resilience, self-esteem, problem-solving, risk-taking, initiating, decision-making, independence, creative and lateral thinking).

- A parent information noticeboard which displays plans for each fortnight's learning and photographs of examples of students at work in a variety of different classes.

- A class information session for parents about how the day and week works and how it includes all the key learning expectations.

- Explanations and descriptions of the approach in detail by leadership and those responsible for school tours and parent interviews.

- Ultranet or website updates and information.

Research and evaluation

Sustained and successful implementation of a new approach requires time and reflection, and will involve successes and challenges throughout the process. The journey will involve moments when people want to give up, and other 'ah ha' moments of realisation and excitement. Part of professional growth and learning for individual teachers, teams and schools as well as the broader education community requires professionals to document the process. This serves a number of significant and helpful purposes:

- evidence of the processes and changes made within a team or school

- identification of the specific challenges which can be used to inform others

- reassurance that progress is being made and tracked

- ideas and suggestions for others

- reminders of what key areas need to be addressed at particular times.

We often suggest additional diagnostic tools can be used in a variety of areas including, social, behavioural, self-esteem and engagement:

- as part of an individual's own professional portfolio

- for use with applications for grants and funds

- as part of professional presentations to other colleagues, conferences.

One of the by-products of working through the implementation process to introduce the WLA is the increased opportunity it provides for staff to reflect on their practices, to revisit and access research and update themselves on teaching and learning strategies and studies. It provides opportunities for staff collectively to discuss, develop stronger shared understandings and to ensure a deeper level of philosophy and pedagogy across an entire school community.

Mapping the journey: A protocol

Change in a school's philosophy and pedagogical approach towards teaching and learning involves a significant and substantial commitment from the school leadership and teaching staff. The change process should be a well-planned and mapped journey. Gathering empirical evidence of any journey is an important part of the planning–evaluating–planning cycle. This evidence should be qualitative and quantitative in nature and should include not just children's outcomes in terms of numeracy and literacy, but build a complete picture of how the change in teaching and learning has influenced the whole child, the teaching group, the leadership and the community.

This protocol is a guideline for how schools can begin to map their journey and collect meaningful and purposeful data. The starting point is most important, as it can be used as the baseline for future projections and reflections; a well-characterised beginning allows for good communication of the true essence of the journey's progression.

Collecting data

Preliminary data capture should include:

- context of school
- rationale for wanting to introduce investigations
- mapping the journey
- current classroom structures and timetable of each day
- current classroom set up (before-and-after photographs are useful).
- reading results as collected by school
- numeracy results as collected by school
- other testing that may be already used by the school or is required by the government.

Additional data that we recommend:

- focus group discussions with parents
- focus group discussions with staff
- focus group discussions with leadership
- diagnostic tools to measure oral language, social skills, engagement, etc. (see recommendations below)
- anecdotal information and feedback from parents and school community including local kindergarten teachers.

Documenting the process of change

This part of the process should include records such as:

- minutes of meetings held with leadership, staff and parents
- number, date and content of professional development sessions
- mentoring experiences
- journal accounts (either electronic, paper or both) which capture the essence of meetings, discussions, changes in planning, timetables and classroom set-up. It is important to have both:
    - a main journal for the school or team
    - journals of notes of mentoring sessions, thoughts, changes, challenges and achievements for each individual teacher.

Additional ideas:

- take lots of photos and videos of children (ensuring first that you have parental permission)
- video some of your team discussions, meetings and mentoring sessions
- video tuning in and reflection time for discussion and professional development among the teaching team.

Diagnostic tool recommendations (see References for full details):

- *ASK-KIDS Inventory for Children* by Dr Laurel Bornholt
- *The Hundred Pictures Naming Test* by John Fisher and Jennifer Glenister
- *Social Skills Improvement System* by Frank Gresham and Stephen Elliott

Summary

- Effective and sustained implementation requires leadership support, direction and knowledge time for preparation, research, evaluation, fact-finding and resourcing.

- Teachers and schools need to understand the basis of the approach is more than adding in some play.

- Time and preparation is needed before the introduction and implementation phase is recommended.

- Extensive and sustained professional development and mentoring by WLA accredited mentors is highly recommended.

- A whole-school approach makes it more sustainable and is most desirable.

- Parents must be informed and educated as to what the approach is and how it facilitates learning.

Chapter 5
Setting up the learning environment

'Childhood is filled with natural wonder and curiosity. The learning environment must reflect a classroom and outdoor space that inspires a sense of wanting to investigate, to find out and to explore.'

Kathy Walker

Introduction

This chapter presents some ideas and examples of how to modify the existing classroom and set up the learning environment to best reflect the philosophy of the WLA.

The environment set-up is informed by child development theory, the intentional planning of the teacher and the current interests of the children and the school community. Getting the environment set up appropriately is one of the keys to engaging the children.

The aim in the WLA classroom is to promote a sense of wonder, exploration, investigation and interest in a rich range of materials, resources and opportunities in which the child can engage. It is referred to as a 'child-centred' classroom and the way equipment and resources are arranged reflects the child as the most important part of the environment.

The environment is described in Reggio Emilia literature as the 'third teacher' (for examples of this concept in action, see www.thethirdteacher.com). It is extremely important that the environment continues to stimulate and scaffold children during their learning at investigation times. Remember that during the years before formal schooling, children will have had access to and been involved in a rich range of learning experiences. The early years of school must extend upon these learning spaces.

The way the learning environment is organised, the range of materials supplied and the types of resources available are essential to the successful implementation of the WLA approach, and to the children being engaged in purposeful and meaningful learning. The learning environment should be set up in such a way that there is no need to constantly pack up and rearrange everything each day.

Teachers sometimes assume that a regular size classroom will not accommodate the WLA approach. In fact, while in an ideal world any classroom should be larger than usual, the WLA works effectively within the indoor and outdoor use of space as long as the environment is established and set up carefully in the first instance.

Classroom organisation and resources

The WLA learning environment reflects some specific characteristics, materials, equipment, furniture and resources, which include:

- the physical space inside the classroom
- individualised floor spaces
- carefully defined and contained learning spaces
- tables used in learning centres.

One of the first things to do is to rearrange the actual indoor space. In a traditional classroom the tables are usually the major feature of the classroom. In the WLA the tables become part of defined areas, rather than being the centrepiece of classrooms.

Practical considerations and implications

Children require an environment that:

- reflects and respects their ideas, interests, strengths and needs
- provides creative and open-ended learning experiences as opposed to cloned art work
- provides opportunities to work or play alone and alongside others
- promotes a sense of authentic choice and belonging
- links learning outside and inside.

Within the learning environment, children need opportunities to:

- self-regulate and self-select
- act independently at times
- pack up and set up responsibilities

- extend experiences into projects at times
- choose from a rich range of materials
- work alongside others if so desired
- enjoy a sense of satisfaction for an ongoing project.

The way the materials are presented, stored and displayed, and how the actual environment is set up, helps children to achieve these opportunities and to work competently and responsibly within the environment.

Creating investigations for children

A key feature of a WLA is to encourage children to keep track of their work. Make sure there are opportunities for writing such as plans, design briefs, and lists so that children can keep up-to-date plans. Making easels with paper and pens, writing tables, clipboards, scrapbooks and individual journals available for children encourages them to take on this role.

Requirements of the indoor learning space

The learning environment is set up with approximately eight learning centres; these learning centres provide experiences for the children to build on developmental skills and their numeracy and literacy in real, relevant and authentic ways. Provocations from the developmental and learning objectives and the emergent and core curriculum are included in the learning centres, and where possible are linked to the intentional teaching. The provocations provide the opportunity for the investigation experiences to be a 'springboard' into the formal teaching.

Dramatic play area

Children need many opportunities for dramatic play. This is a major way in which oral language and a range of other literacy and numeracy skills are developed as well as problem solving, decision making, persistence, creative and lateral thinking.

It should be noted that dramatic play occurs in many different areas of the learning environment, not just in a defined dramatic play area, but it is important and useful to have a defined dramatic play space which can facilitate a wide range of concepts and understandings. This is usually in a corner, and large enough for four or five children to work and create. It can also be encouraged through the use of dramatic props such as building blocks, Lego, doll's houses, cosy corners to investigate or 'pull-apart' tables with old computers.

Examples of dramatic play include:

- supermarket
- post office
- airport
- hospital
- shop
- milk bar.

Children will also initiate ideas for dramatic play that may be based on a discussion with the teacher. Teachers may set up a dramatic play concept based on the interests and ideas of the children or introduce a particular dramatic play focus depending upon some of the issues or ideas the teacher wishes to promote.

Dramatic play is one of the major strategies for promoting rich oral language for both children who have English as a first language and also for children who have English as a second language. The language in dramatic play is rich, purposeful and authentic. Children are highly motivated and engaged and the vocabulary, grammar, articulation and listening skills are all highly evident in dramatic play.

Many numeracy and literacy skills are also enhanced and promoted through dramatic play. The provocations intentionally included in the learning areas will facilitate the development of these skills; for example clocks, appointment pads, books, newspapers, fax machines. Examples of these are given in Chapter 7.

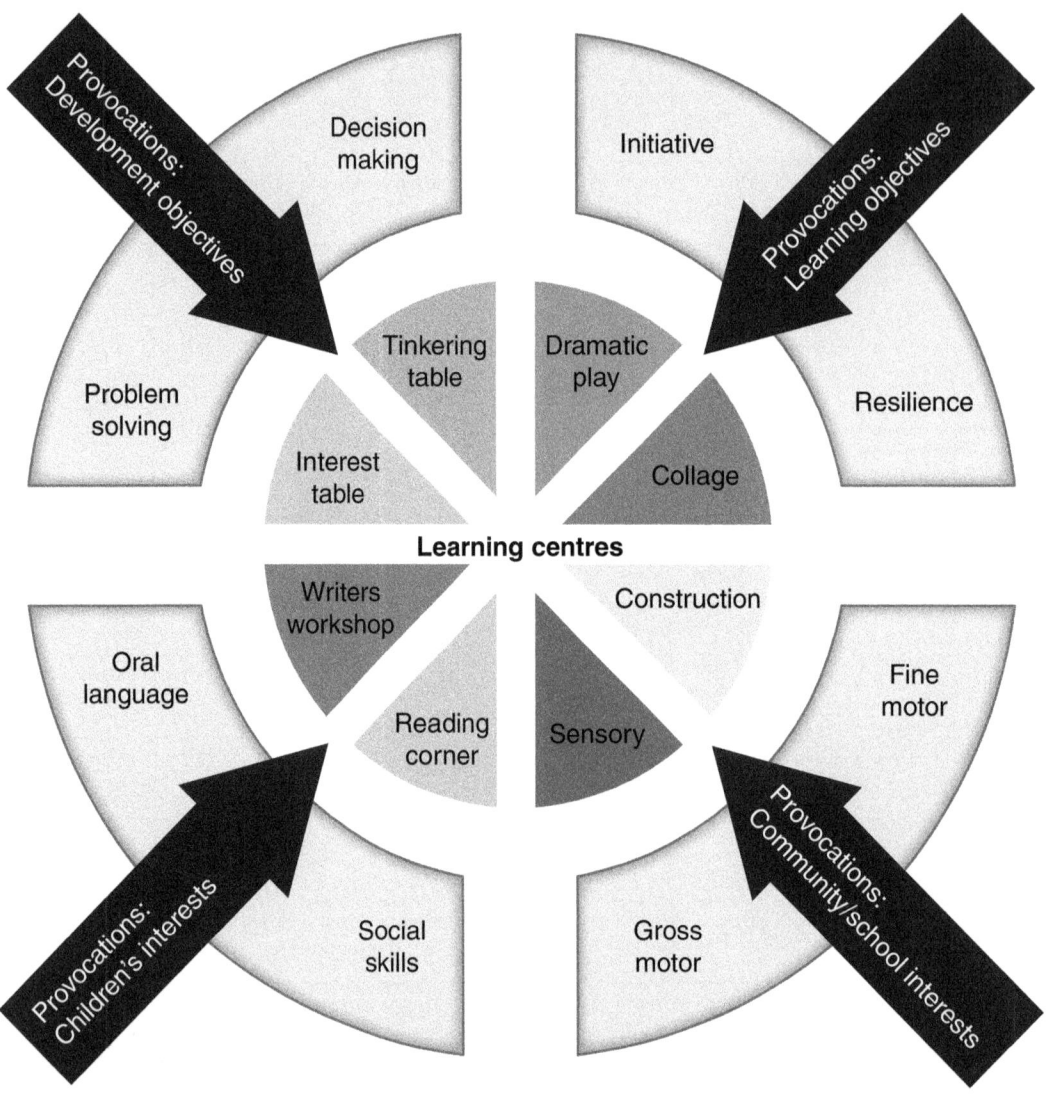

Figure 5.1 Learning centres, provocations and skills developed

Sensory play area

These areas are important for children and can also be set up outside the classroom. A sensory area provides fine motor and hand–eye practice, but additionally allows children to experience creativity and to be in tune with not just their thinking and academic skills but the sensory perception areas as well. At times these can link directly to a literacy experience or they may simply be a means unto themselves, which children may then extend. Sensory play may include:

- clay
- playdough
- water
- mud
- sand with a fragrance
- dirt with natural materials such as pine cones.

These can often be in small trays or buckets to facilitate individual or small groups of children engaging in the experience.

Collage/creating area

The collage area provides rich opportunities for a never ending range of creativity, projects, experimentation with materials and where much literacy and numeracy occurs. The area is usually two tables but not joined together, perhaps L shaped. This enables children to work in smaller groups.

Always provide access for children to a range of collage materials. These need to be stored and don't all have to be available each day, but children need to be aware there is a supply of different collage materials.

Displaying and presenting the materials needs to create a sense of invitation, order, grouping and organisation, rather than just having everything stored in a large box or container which children cannot see into. It also helps children to respect the materials and makes it easier for them to pack away.

The range of collage materials should also reflect variety and include, at different times, some of the following suggestions:

- natural materials such as gumnuts, pine cones, leaves, flowers, pebbles or feathers
- boxes of different sizes
- cardboard
- coloured paper
- cotton wool
- buttons
- ribbons.

The list is endless. Utilising parents to collect resources and joining somewhere like a reverse art shop, as well as getting local shopkeepers to collect off-cuts for instance, is invaluable.

Writing workshop table

A table with pens, papers, scissors and work-in-progress signs helps to create a learning environment that children associate with writing and reading as an integral and purposeful tool in their investigations. Signs around this area, with letter formations modelled and with all sorts of paper and pens accessible to children, invites them to use writing and documenting within context and not just at a specific 'writing' time.

Reading area

Reading areas are used for relaxing, reading, researching, sharing information and storytelling. They should be quiet, attractive and defined spaces, which also reflect an exciting or inviting place for children to visit. Some teachers create particular spaces for reading areas, using netting, tents, cushions and sofas.

Reading spaces should hold a range of non-fiction as well as fiction books that children can use in their research. Children's own books, reflecting their projects, can be displayed as authentic and quality books for other children to share and read together.

Computers and technology

The WLA embraces the use of a range of technologies (including the use of computers) as long as they are tools used for learning and projects and not aimless play. Computers are used in the following ways:

- creatively for designs and plans
- for documenting work and writing stories
- for reflection through the development of PowerPoint presentations
- for researching
- for creating animation and stories.

Computers are not to be used for games. Often, children who most need oral language experience and practice and hands-on social interaction are the ones who gravitate toward the computer for games. This is to be discouraged.

Construction and manipulative equipment

Children construct knowledge and understandings through hands-on creating. These experiences are an integral part of the WLA play approach. Children need opportunities to develop, plan and represent ideas, and to reflect, map out, construct and complete their designs. These may at times relate to some particular part of a project, or may just be something that is useful and relevant to the child on that particular day.

Ensure there are resources such as Lego or Mobilo for children to work with. Provision of shelving or display spaces for works-in-progress encourage children to return to, extend and build on some of their projects. It may be that photographs are taken of the works and used for pages in a class or student book.

Spaces for construction can be defined with masking tape on the floor in squares or circles or with mats as described below.

Blocks

Blocks are one of the most versatile and constructive tools for children to use. Design work, planning, actual construction, and the extension of dramatic play into the block area is rich and filled with many opportunities for the teacher to scaffold numeracy and literacy.

Blocks are also very effective outside and can link to an easel where a design brief might need to be completed before the construction stage commences. Blocks are highly recommended.

Individual mats

These mats, approximately 1 m x 1 m, help to define spaces for individual children. At times children may wish to join them together to form larger groups. They can also be used outside so children have something comfortable to sit on as they work. In an average class size (23 children), each room could have 5–10 mats. They are easily stacked and stored.

Mats encourage children to work either in solitary, parallel or associative play, which as discussed in Chapter 2, are important for all children.

Individual spaces or cosy corners

In their early years, children still like time to work and play on their own. It actually helps with concentration and attending to tasks, and limits interruptions from others. These areas reflect the philosophy that all children, spending up to six or more hours together in the same space, require the respect of sometimes being able to have more of their own personal space.

Placing a few cosy corners around the room, perhaps defined by some netting material or noticeboards, helps give a retreat and some quiet space for children's investigations. These cosy corners are usually set up with just one small table and one chair or cushion to sit on. They can incorporate a range of experiences, such as a tinkering table (perhaps with an old computer, typewriter or television), a doll's house, interest tables, nature tables and buzzers and batteries.

Group time area

Children need time to meet together, to share ideas, to reflect, to engage in explicit instruction sessions and to spend time chatting with the teacher.

Each room requires some space where the children can come together. It doesn't always have to be at the front of the room and teachers are encouraged to set up the room first, and then find the space for group time.

Additional suggestions for classroom organisation and set-up

It is a good idea to attempt to minimise the number of things around the room, so as to avoid an over-stimulating classroom. However, some of these suggestions may be useful:

- a noticeboard, pegs or letterboxes for children to write notes to each other

- clipboards (children love them!)

- scrapbooks for each child (to hold their design briefs, made before or after the child constructs)

- displays at child level rather than adult level

- signs that promote independence, responsibility and pride in work, for example, work-in-progress signs.

Requirements of the outdoor learning space

The WLA views outdoor space as equal to indoor space, and extremely important in learning for children. If possible, establishing places to learn outside is a great way to ease the pressure within the classroom. Many children, particularly boys, work more constructively and productively outside.

Setting up an environment that allows children to move more freely and comfortably helps to ease some of the behaviour disruptions that can occur when children are working very closely together. It is desirable that children can move between inside and outside during the day and that the learning is viewed by them as being inside and outside.

Some schools are lucky in that they have direct access to outside space, with veranda areas or courtyards. Schools that don't have these easily accessible spaces may have to provide more limited time outside.

Outdoor learning provides the opportunity for sensory experiences such as water, sand and mud. Having 1 m × 1 m mats to work on outside helps children to be comfortable and to construct and build on a surface if they wish to. Mats also help to define spaces. All experiences that are provided inside can also be provided outside.

Painting easels

Painting easels are an effective tool for improving bilateral coordination, and both gross and fine motor skills. They are useful for promoting oral language, thinking planning, and describing colour and shape concepts. They are also a convenient tool for children's design briefs, mapping and planning experiences.

A variety of mediums can be provided at the easels other than just paint. Pasting with a range of materials at the easels provides a different perspective in which children can explore and experiment.

It is preferable to include two easels side by side so that they can be either a social and language experience for children or a solitary experience.

Table and chairs for sitting and talking

It is useful to have one table and a couple of chairs outside so that children can sit and chat with each other from time to time. They may do some group planning or design briefs before they commence their work.

Woodwork bench

This is an exciting and highly creative experience in which children can engage. The use of tools, the practice of building and constructing, taking responsibility, planning, designing and linking their woodwork to literacy and numeracy are some of the benefits of woodwork.

Fine motor skills, oral language as children work alongside each other and other key skills including problem solving, perseverance and lateral thinking, are all promoted in this experience.

Strategies for outdoors and duty of care issues

Ensuring that children are safe, supervised and engaged in productive play and learning occurs more easily than might be anticipated by teachers who are used to the learning occurring only inside the classroom. Because children are actively engaged in experiences that are authentic and in which they are interested, they are more likely to work productively and less likely to move away from the area.

Duty of care issues are often raised as a concern with outdoor leaning. Schools need to work through ways in which to overcome these issues. There are many strategies that can be implemented by the teacher to help ensure the children are safe outdoors:

- children have to sign in and out of the classroom, and the teacher has to co-sign

- a timer is set for 15 minutes and children have to re-negotiate more outside time with the teacher if required

- equipment is placed close to doorways making observation easier

- if parent helpers are part of the program they may be able to help supervise the outdoor areas.

> **Suggested process for teachers reorganising the learning environment**
>
> - *Take out all tables and clear the classroom.*
>
> - *With the room empty, plan how the core learning centres will be set out.*
>
> - *Place tables individually, rather than in large groups in the centre of the room.*
>
> - *Use dividers, noticeboards, shelves or cupboards to help define contained areas.*
>
> - *Use 1 m × 1 m mats to help define and individualise spaces for children to work.*
>
> - *Dramatic play space needs to be large enough to accommodate four or five children at a time.*
>
> - *Reading area must be inviting, comfortable, sometimes exciting.*

Literacy and numeracy

While Chapter 9 discusses examples of how literacy and numeracy link into the WLA, the list below gives a brief overview of some of the materials and resources that can help to extend and scaffold the experiences within literacy and numeracy.

In a number of areas (including block play and dramatic play areas), provide writing paper, clipboards, lists, notepads, journals, portfolios, easels with paper and pens for design briefs, and a writer's table with pens, pencils, paper, stamps, letters and envelopes.

Promoting creativity and ideas

Using a rich range of writing and drawing materials, pasting and construction are the key ingredients that promote children's oral language, literacy, numeracy, creativity and initiative. The use of cloned art work, stencilled ideas, pre-drawn ideas and colouring-in sheets is unnecessary.

Ensure that materials can be mixed together. For example, placing Lego, animals or writing materials alongside blocks helps promote a richer investigation.

Promoting persistence

An important part of the work of children is to return to it, to persist, to work further on some of their tasks and to feel a sense of pride in their attempts. The provision of some special display space or shelving for storing works in progress is important to children. They are encouraged to respect each other's work as well as to continue their own work, and not just work at something or complete something in 10 minutes.

Some key points for consideration:

- Not all children must have a table to sit at or a chair to sit on.

- Play and work stations should remain where they are, and not require packing away each day.

- Provide space for displays of investigations.

- The nature of the experiences should not require an adult to be present in order for the experiences to be productive or for the children to be able to work on them. For example, avoid sewing or threading experiences unless you have an additional adult to assist.

Table 5.1 Checklist for setting up the learning environment

General
Learning centres are clearly defined and the room is not dominated by a table in the centre
Learning centres are simple, tidy, engaging and linked to developmentally appropriate practice
There is a broad and rich range of learning centres that stimulate children's language and thinking skills and link the experiences to literacy, numeracy and other learning across the curriculum
There are print-rich experiences at all learning centres
Learning centres include a writing workshop and reading corner, as well as areas for collage, sensory, construction and dramatic play
Activities are open ended
Dramatic play
Dress-up clothes are organised, hanging and visible
There is a range of clothing that avoids costumes (no superheroes)
There are real-life items, such as phones, faxes, plates, pots, calculators and computer keyboards
There is enough space for at least four children
Clipboards and paper are provided for writing opportunities
There is a selection of texts relative to the area, such as menus, recipe books, phone books and appointment books
Collage
There is a wide range of resources that promote creatively and imagination
There is a selection of natural items
Items are well stocked and clearly organised (feathers, sticks, cotton balls, bark, leaves, pipe cleaners, paper plates)
There is a selection of texts available relevant to emergent and core curriculum (books about making puppets or making masks)
A selection of design briefs is available
Sensory
The small area is designed for one or two children
There is a rich range of environmental texts (zoo animals with zoo map, animal fiction and nonfiction texts, photos)
Clipboards and paper are provided for writing opportunities
Range of experiences are possible (water, sand, mud, water crystals, soap flakes, music, scents, different textures)
Construction
There are wooden blocks, Lego, Mobilo or other construction materials
There are additional items to support investigation (cars, people, animals)
Clipboards and paper are provided for writing opportunities
There are posters and books relative to the area
The centre is placed in an area of the room that allows space for construction and allows constructions to be left as work in progress
Reading corner
The area is inviting and cosy and in a quiet part of the room
There is a wide selection of good quality texts including some related to the emergent curriculum
Books are displayed at children's level preferably with front cover facing
Writing workshop
There is a wide range of writing implements
There are additional resources (staplers, hole punches)
There are a range of papers (lined, coloured, white, different sizes) that are well-organised and accessible
There are resources to support writing (dictionary, thesaurus, high frequency word chart, children's names, alphabet chart, example of text type)

Summary

- The learning space is both indoors and outdoors. If outdoors is not possible, the indoor space can accommodate most of the experiences.

- The learning environment must reflect individual spaces as well as contained and defined spaces that do not need to be dominated by tables.

- Ensure a full range of different experiences is provided for, including dramatic play, sensory play, writing, reading and construction.

- Avoid having too many pieces of work hanging from the ceiling and over-stimulating children with excessive visual stimuli.

- The provision of open-ended materials promotes creativity.

- Cloned art work, colouring-in, and cloned worksheets are not used.

- Literacy and numeracy are linked explicitly to play through the provision of particular materials.

- Ensure children have access to a full range of materials so the teacher does not have to be interrupted repeatedly during each session.

Tuning in

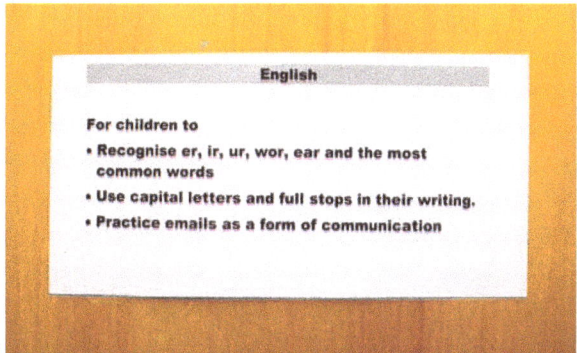

During tuning in, the teacher models and scaffolds the learning intentions.

Learning intentions and the focus child roster are displayed (in large font and on A3 paper) for parents and children.

The teacher models learning intentions during tuning in. The two-week focus child roster, and the focus children, reporter and photographer for the day are on the whiteboard.

A child contributes at tuning in time, linking to the stated literacy learning objectives.

Reporter and photographer

In the early years, the reporter role generally involves writing and drawing pictures. In Grades 1 and 2 reporter activities can include making videos, collecting data and interviewing visitors.

The photographer role provides the opportunity to develop skills such as reflection, timing, perspective taking and linking to documentation.

Reflection time

Tuning in and reflection time are conducted as a conversation between the focus children, reporter, photographer and the rest of the class. The teacher scaffolds the children and models the language of learning during the conversation.

The teacher unpacks the intentional teacher-directed tasks for the reporter and photographer during reflection time.

The teacher scaffolds a focus child and unpacks the learning related to the authentic interests of the child developed during tuning in.

Work in progress

The work in progress signs provide the opportunity for the children to develop extended engagement in their investigations over a longer period of time.

Construction learning centre

Children work together and independently, all with intention about their investigations or in the teacher-directed role as photographer.

Boys in the block-building area are developing their skills in design, oral language, planning and spatial awareness.

Design briefs are used intentionally. Initially they may be undertaken after construction. In Grades 1 and 2 they would be undertaken before construction. Design briefs develop the children's skills in planning, designing and following procedures.

Dramatic play learning centre

Dramatic play involves real-life experiences in perspective taking, role play, rehearsal, writing, performance, and collaborating.

Using real-life materials adds to oral language development.

These children are in a 'restaurant', taking orders for the meal. Skills include writing, speaking, working together, lists and ordering.

Dramatic play with props and provocations provides the opportunity for children to be exposed to numeracy and literacy in real, relevant and meaningful ways.

Outdoor dramatic play can involve construction, design, planning, oral language and collaboration.

Including telephones, fax machines, writing pads, label and textbooks along with real-life props can promote thinking, oral language and collaboration.

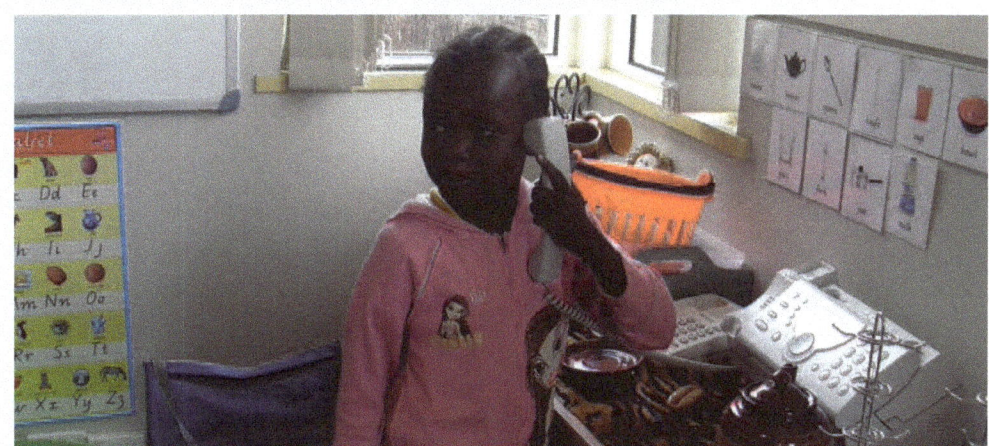

Investigations can involve making costumes and props then using these in dramatic play.

Sensory learning centre

The teacher intentionally includes provocations that will link play in the sensory areas to more formal learning.

These link sensory experiences with text, and spaces are defined using natural materials.

Taking learning outside: Sensory experiences can link with intentional teaching about measuring, liquids, fluid flow and collaboration.

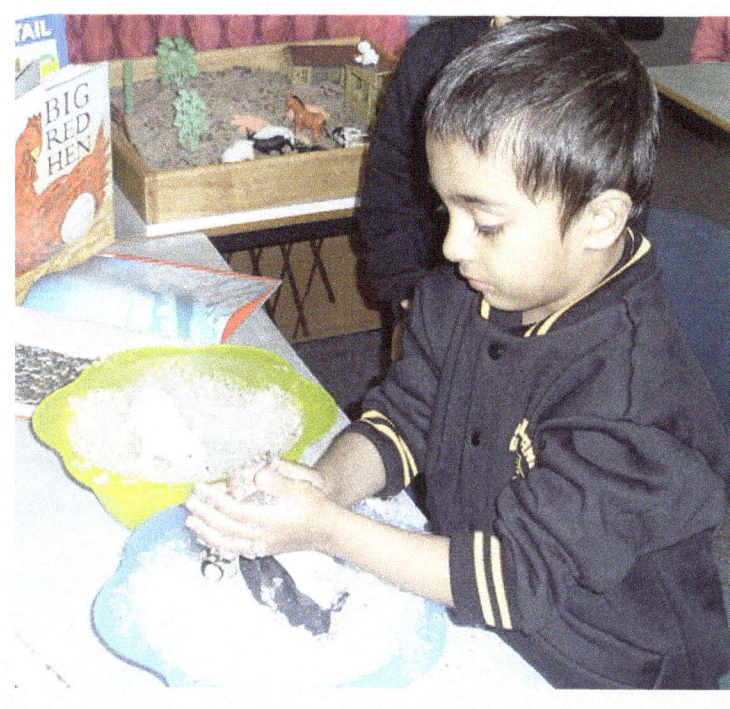

A clay area can demonstrate a broad range of utensils to promote fine motor skills, imagination, creativity and oral language.

A diverse, print-rich range of materials and provocations link text, sensory concepts and oral language together in specific learning centres.

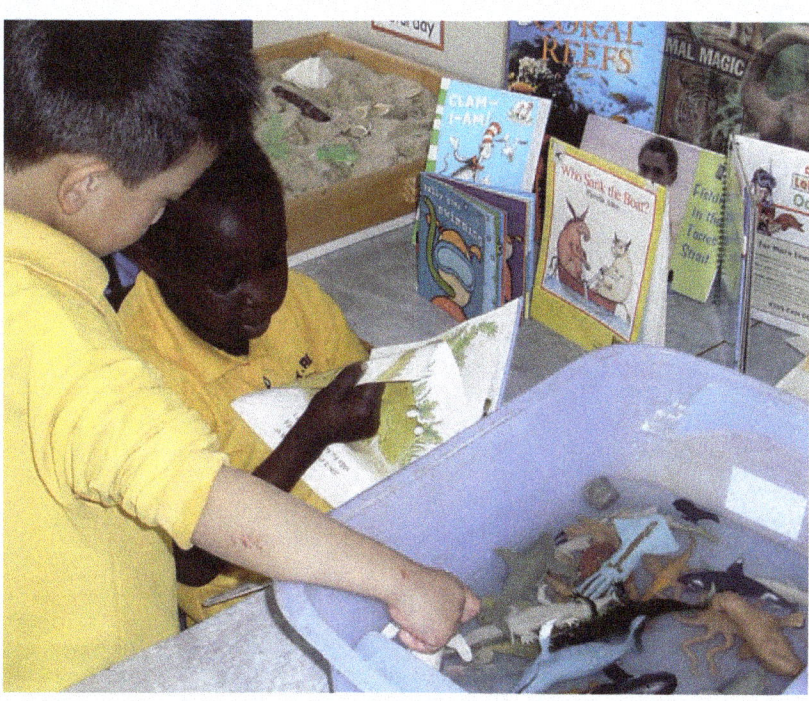

Using a range of objects such as fish, animals, sand and pinecones can expose children to a broad range of experiences and concepts.

Reading learning centre

Reading and sharing can happen outside and separate from group reading time. It is important to link reading to everyday life.

Collage learning centre

The collage area is always tidy, well categorised and provides a visual provocation for the children's ideas.

Natural materials predominate and there will never be any stencils or cloned work. Where possible add provocations to the collage area related to the emergent and core curriculums.

Painting on the vertical plane promotes a variety of ways to represent feelings, thoughts and ideas.

Interest learning centres

Interest tables are not themed or based on topics. They provide opportunities for a diverse range of science or nature experiences for the children.

A music station can expand by adding instruments, enriching the environment with many of the arts and music experiences.

Outdoor learning

Using real objects and active participation to link to text, stories and comprehension.

Communication board

The communication board displays the statement of intent (A3), learning intentions, two-week focus children roster and photographs of investigations making the explicit and intentional links to the learning intentions.

Chapter 6

A typical day using the Walker Learning Approach

'It is the supreme art of the teacher to awaken joy in creative expression and knowledge.'

Albert Einstein

Introduction

This chapter describes how a typical day transpires using WLA. What follows is a set of ideas, based on a range of schools that use the approach and some key principles that are the basis for how to integrate and embed the approach into the learning environment. As stated earlier in the book, the approach does not attempt to squeeze in a bit of play on top of the existing busy day. It becomes the major pedagogical tool for teaching and learning and engaging children in active, hands-on learning.

A typical day or week of the WLA can be 'chunked' into broad categories of (i) investigations; (ii) formal teaching and (iii) other programs/specialist groups. Despite these categories, it is important that investigations and formal teaching have continuity and are connected, rather than being seen as separate entities. Each teacher and classroom is encouraged to reflect and develop their own typical day alongside the key principles and core elements of the WLA.

Morning session

At least four mornings a week the children start their day with investigations. There are four distinct core elements of the investigations:

1. tuning in for the learning of the day;
2. investigating—child initiated and adult directed concrete hands-on activities
3. reflection—scaffolding the experiences of the investigation to link with the current learning objectives
4. resetting the environment for the rest of the day and investigations the next day

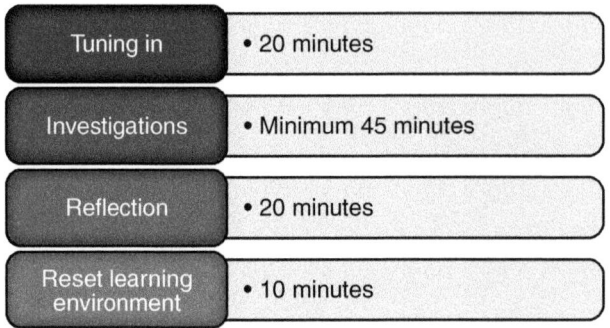

Figure 6.2   Outline of investigations (≥ 95 minutes)

Children sit together to reflect on prior day's learning, and investigations. They may discuss events, birthdays, experiences or points of interest.

Think creatively about some of the practical issues that often take up too much time and lead to the children disengaging. Try to avoid these as much as you can. Taking the roll can be one experience to promote children's literacy. Ask each child to mark themselves off.

Show and tell is not part of this time; in fact show and tell is not necessary at any time as there are many other times and opportunities being provided for sharing, listening and talking together.

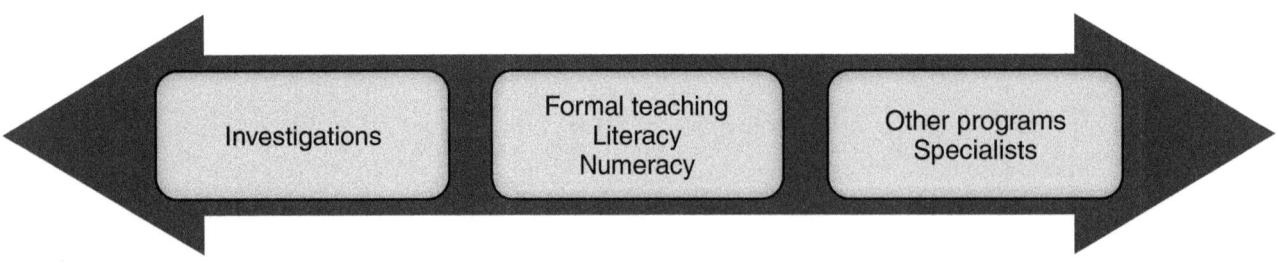

Figure 6.1   A typical day or week in the WLA classroom

Tuning in

Helping to focus the children on their learning from the previous day and directing them into the work for the morning is the major aim of this first meeting time. This is a particularly important time to set the tone and pace for the whole day. The teacher models the language of learning consistent with the intention mapped out in the learning intentions. It is tuning in for the learning for the whole day, not just for investigations.

You might use some photographs from the previous day to help tune children into some of their projects or play. You might use a list on a whiteboard or the daily record sheet from the day before (a pro forma is located on the CD).

If sharing a large space with two or more groups, all tuning in and reflections must occur with children's own home groups.

It is helpful for the teacher to break the tuning in into four key sections that in total last about 20 minutes.

1. Welcome:
   - general chat, the roll, lunch orders, day of the week, seasons, etc.

2. Tuning in for the learning for the day:
   - a quick revision of current literacy and numeracy learning—children may provide examples
   - reminding children of the key learning intentions and timetable of the day.

3. Three focus children and the reporter/photographer each stand up to be tuned in:
   - discussions with each about what they are working on or thinking of doing (teacher modelling intention)
   - in most situations teacher honours and respects the choice of the focus child but may scaffold or set expectations

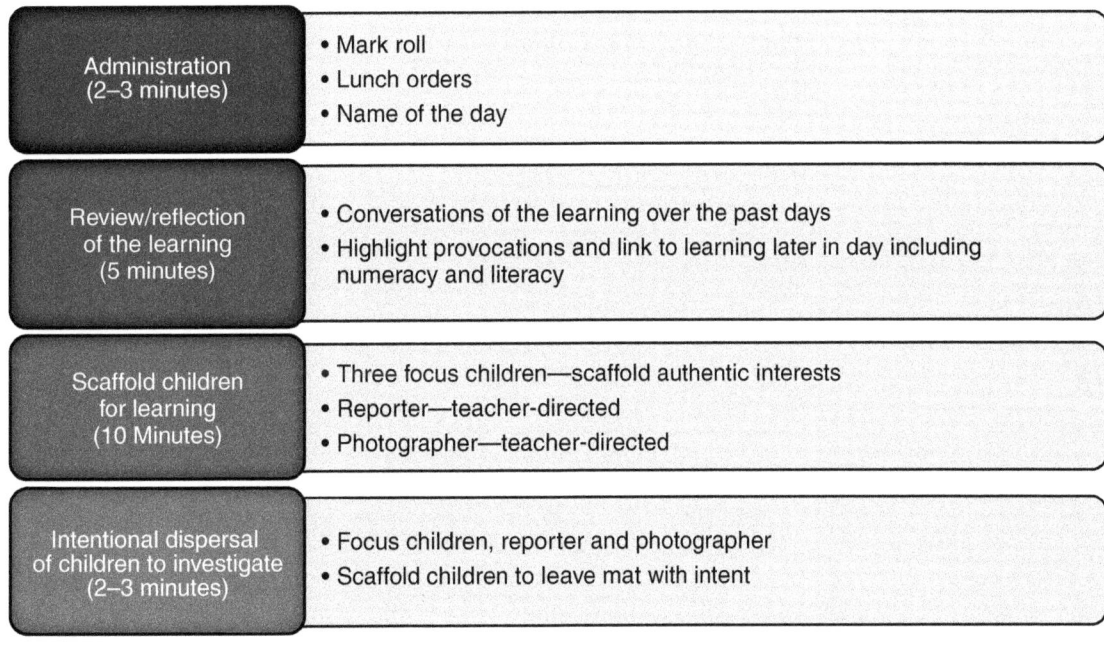

Figure 6.3 Tuning in schedule (20 minutes)

- teacher can set the agenda and expectations with the reporter and photographer.

4. Dispersal:

 - focus children, reporter and photographer can go first, then the rest of the children are helped to identify where and what they may be working on or what experience they will start with

 - the idea here is that there is still some intention and thinking, not just rushing off the mat.

Investigation time

The children's investigations take place after tuning in and require a minimum of 45 minutes. In the first part of investigations the teacher will scaffold the focus children, reporter and photographer. In the second part of investigations the teacher will scaffold and observe children who may need support or extending.

Children will be dispersed to their choice or teacher's choice of work or learning area to continue with work from the previous day or to commence something new. Some children may be directed to particular areas depending upon the teacher's scaffolding. Some may have to complete a design brief or plan their work before getting underway with their investigation or project. This might be done in an individual work folder or journal. Some may have to write about their project from the day before or map out what they intend to do next.

The teacher may choose to watch or participate in the investigation, observing language, literacy and numeracy skills. (See Chapter 8 on observation, assessment and planning for further details.) The children may work on their related tasks for one or two hours or more. Flexibility with a snack is allowed when the individual child feels hungry or thirsty. It is not necessary to wait until a formal morning recess.

Reflection

Reflection time is a critical aspect of the WLA pedagogy. You can never run investigations without having a reflection time. Reflection time is not show and tell. Reflection time helps to identity the learning that has occurred during the session and most importantly is a springboard and link back into the literacy and numeracy that is occurring for the rest of the day.

Reflection has three key elements making up about 20 minutes in total.

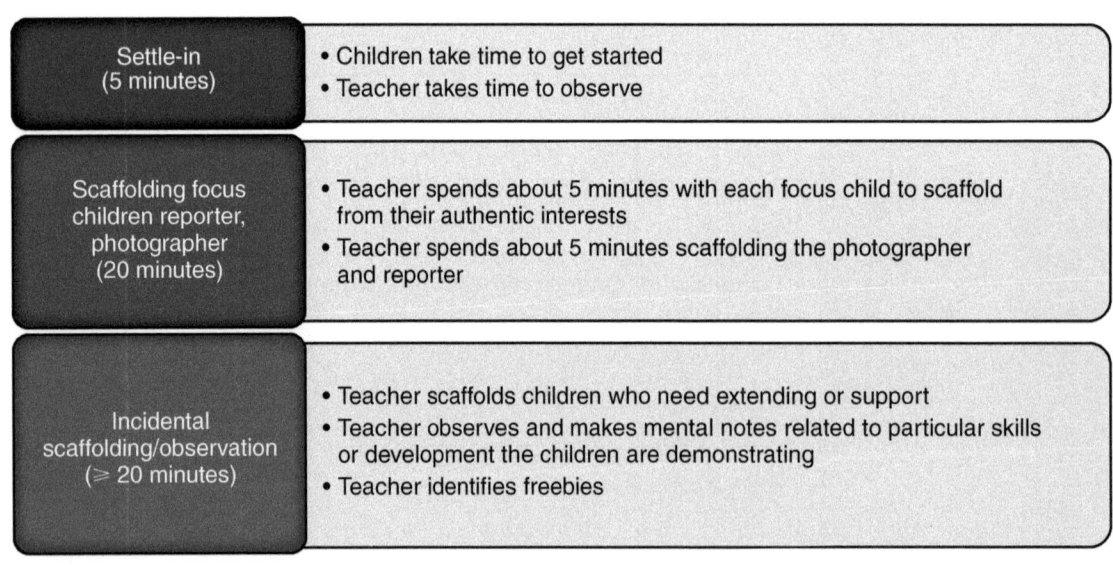

Figure 6.4 Investigation time (≥ 45 minutes)

- Reporter/photographer:
  - reports back on task they were assigned and what they learned
  - children are encouraged to respond, to comment and ask questions.
- Focus children:
  - report back on their learning and work
  - teacher highlights skills or learning that have occurred
  - children are encouraged to ask questions and make comments.
- Freebies—one or two children who have either:
  - demonstrated a skill that happens to link with literacy, numeracy or other learning intentions.
  - demonstrated an interest, skill or behaviour that doesn't necessarily link to current plans but is just a great moment to capture, share and model with the children.
  - Freebies can be used either at the end of reflection time or at the commencement of a literacy/numeracy session to highlight a skill that links to what is currently being taught.
- Organising and packing up for the rest of the day's learning:
  - this is meant to be a relaxed, purposeful, unhurried experience for the children where they are reflecting, organising and packing up
  - we often suggest only half the children actually do the packing up while the rest may read, organise the work in progress shelf or make lists of what other materials or resources they need for the next day
  - the key here is that it should not be a rushed, noisy experience. Children need a quiet transition from investigations to the rest of the day's learning.

Tuning in and reflection time are the key non-negotiable aspects of the WLA each day.

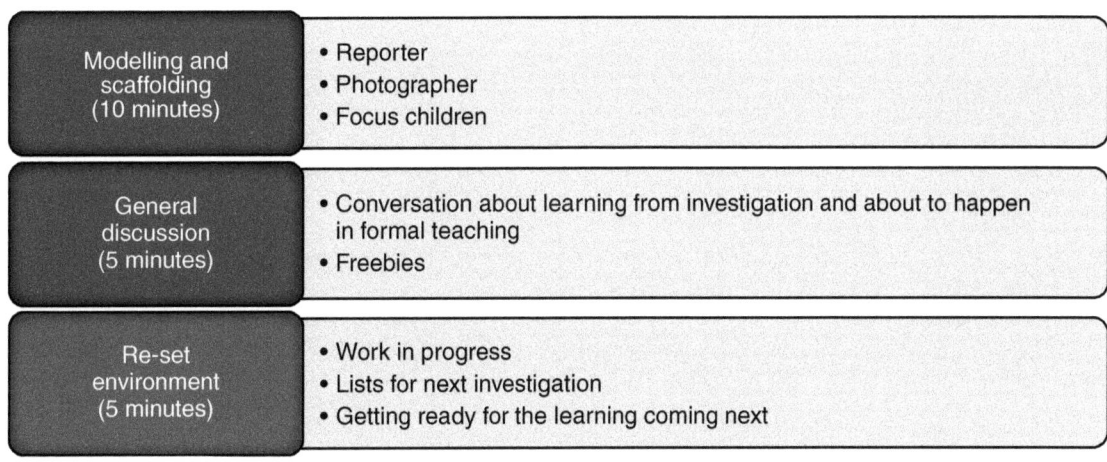

Figure 6.5 Reflection schedule (20 minutes)

Table 6.1 Example of teacher scaffolding

Person	Dialogue	Comment
Teacher	Abraham, you are a focus child today. Would you please come up and tell us what you will be working on?	The teacher always uses terminology such as 'working on' and 'investigating' rather than 'playing with'.
Abraham	I am going to play with my Pokémon cards.	This is his authentic interest.
Teacher	Abraham, I know you really love your Pokémon cards, but we have a rule that we are not to play with Pokémon cards during investigations. But I have an idea. I have some blank cards in the store: maybe you would like to make your own Pokémon deck?	The teacher knows that Abraham loves Pokémon cards. She would have checked the planning documents before tuning in and would have developed some ideas about Abraham's interests and how they could be extended. The blank cards were one idea. This is intentional teaching.
Abraham	Oh, that sounds a good idea ... but how would I do that?	This is where the teacher now scaffolds Abraham, modelling the language of learning while facilitating discussion between Abraham and the rest of the group. This not only helps Abraham develop his ideas and intent, it also helps the other children develop their ideas and intent.
Teacher	Well, why don't you tell us about your Pokémon cards and what you like about them?	The teach helps the child to unpack ideas, to think about what components he likes about the cards, and in doing so identify what he will do with the blank cards.
Abraham	Each Pokémon has its own picture and character, and its own attack and defence scores.	
Teacher	I see a lot of writing and bright pictures on your cards ... and some very scary characters. So how might we use the blank cards to make our own Pokémon cards?	
A second child in the class	Why don't you make up your own special Pokémon characters? You could give them names and draw them.	
A third child in the class	Yes, and you could give them attack and defence scores! I can help you.	
Second child	Yes, I can help you too, Abraham.	
		In this class the three children worked together for three weeks. Not only did they make their own Pokémon deck with their own characters, they also developed their own game, wrote out the rules of the game and then taught the game to other students.
		It could have been easy for the teacher to say, 'Put the Pokémon cards away and work on something else.' This is the easy option. The teacher with excellent planning and documentation and intentional teaching was able to scaffold Abraham from his authentic interest and provide the opportunity for deep emersion in numeracy, literacy, fine motor control, cooperation, communication, writing and comprehension. The teacher was also able to model the language of learning.

Instruction throughout the rest of the day

Throughout the day, the teacher will use small clinic groups and/or whole groups for formal instruction in particular aspects of writing, reading or maths concepts. The teacher can use examples from the investigations as a lead-in to the literacy or numeracy sessions. For example, instead of writing on Monday morning, 'What I did on the weekend', children can be invited to write about their investigations, their feelings or their explorations.

Instruction and explicit teaching can also be flexible. At times, some teachers may have the intention of modelling a particular letter, but a child has asked about a letter through one of their projects. There is nothing to stop the teacher using that letter for instruction because it is relevant and immediate.

The goal is to actively engage children and motivate them in learning and skill instruction through their experiences and interests as much as possible. Children are much more likely to want to write when it is about something that is of authentic and immediate interest to them.

Handwriting, spelling and reading are all areas of learning that the WLA embraces, and that at times, whole group instruction time will model and teach. The children's investigations serve as the basis for many of the skills and explicit teaching experiences that the teacher can use to engage the children.

Rotations

Rotations are not necessary. Due to their brain development and concentration, young children require at least 15 minutes to become engaged in their learning and experiences. They also require time to wander off and to return to their tasks so that they can complete them with a sense of meaningful achievement. Rotations do not often give children enough time to engage, to explore, to become motivated and interested, to create, discover or extend themselves. In fact, children often complain of rotations that 'We never got to finish anything'.

Literacy and numeracy

Daily literacy and numeracy instruction times are still necessary. Aspects of literacy and numeracy are embedded into investigations but of course taught and reinforced through explicit clinic instruction times that can occur at any time throughout the day. Many of the skills and learning intentions set for literacy are embedded in children's investigations, and others can be modelled and instructed through explicit instruction clinics or whole group classes. The goal in the WLA is to embed literacy and numeracy opportunities into investigations and then to use these experiences as a springboard into formal instruction. But classes will still retain discrete times for formal instruction in literacy and numeracy. Young children in their early years must still be formally introduced to actual skills including, handwriting, letter sounds and recognition of letters, etc.

The language used in relation to literacy changes from 'doing literacy in the morning', to learning a range of literacy and numeracy skills every day, at different times and in different ways. Formal instruction is still required but not locked into the same time, and divorced totally from the interests and needs of the children.

Overview

Each day (or at least four days a week) has a mix of active engagement through investigations, clinic groups, whole group instruction, formal instruction in literacy and numeracy and specialist classes. While routine and predictability is important for young children, each day can vary according to the group dynamic, the level of tiredness or interest of the children, practical considerations such as weather, and the scaffolding or experiences that the teacher wishes to pursue.

Topics are not required and not used in the WLA and as explained in detail in Chapter 5, any particular community events, or specific focus of content that a teacher may wish to include, can be integrated into the range and mix of experiences that can engage children. A separate integrated studies unit is not required and not used.

Understandings, skills, concepts, ideas and research skills are all promoted through the use of both children's interests and the interests that are introduced and integrated by the teacher. This does not mean that a school can't introduce particular areas of interest, but the planning and children's interests, the learning objectives and developmental domain objectives are the starting point, rather than a topic or unit of work. (See Chapter 7 for details on planning.)

The teacher's role

Teaching and learning through investigations

- *Teacher plans learning and development intentions.*
- *Teacher provides a variety of learning opportunities through a range of play materials and equipment.*
- *Child engages in the process.*
- *Teacher observes or participates.*
- *Teacher scaffolds learning experiences through investigations.*
- *Teacher extends, intervenes or scaffolds the child as emergent interests, skills and understandings are identified.*
- *Further clinic groups or formal teaching of skills or concepts extended from investigations and children's understandings are carried out.*
- *Investigations continue and are modified, renewed, extended or started afresh.*

The importance of the adult as the scaffold in learning

The teacher's role in the WLA is a major one for modelling, observing, building explicit teaching skills into some of the interests and investigations of the children, knowing when and how to extend children and when to leave them in their current investigation.

The term 'scaffold' is worth revisiting. A scaffold, in building terms, is to provide a support around a current construction and to provide opportunities for further growth, building, construction and achievement. Scaffolding by the teacher occurs in a variety of ways in the WLA:

- Through observation and knowledge of children's current interests, skills and maturation. This assists the teacher to plan accordingly and to build opportunities for practice or instruction based on where the children are currently at, not where we might expect them to be. (Chapters 7 and 8 provide examples of how to do this for each child.)

- Through modelling explicit instruction based on current interests of children.

- In providing ideas or suggestions for taking current interests into new, perhaps unexplored or unknown areas or experiences.

- Linking literacy and numeracy experiences to the projects and investigations of the children. For example, when children are making a restaurant, scaffolding would link some of the experiences to making money, counting profits made, writing recipes, menus, advertising the restaurant

- Encouraging the reflection and sharing of ideas with other children for imitation and modelling with each other.

- Ensuring a relationship with children, based on listening to their language and interests and building authentic discussions with them.

- Providing a wide range of materials and resources that are accessible for children.

- Working one on one with each focus child, reporter and photographer.

The key is that children are given long, uninterrupted time to engage, to work and investigate each day and that explicit teaching instruction links as much as possible to the work and investigations of the children.

Integrated studies and separate times for a theme or topic are not required and can not be used in this approach. If particular or additional issues or concepts are being introduced to the children, they are introduced alongside the children's project and interest areas so that the learning is truly integrated and children can see links that are meaningful and relevant to their own lives.

The key is to unblock the day, to ensure less segregated learning, and for children to see their investigations as a major part of their learning and work, not as a novelty, free time or undirected time.

Summary

- Each day provides a mix of, investigations and formal teaching instruction.

- Children come together to plan, discuss, reflect and to be directed into their investigations.

- Sometimes children may have a choice in their work and other times the teacher will direct or scaffold the child in a particular area of learning or investigation.

- Group times are not lengthy and promote active discussion, reflection and planning with children.

- Photos can be used with children to help with reflection and further planning.

- There is still a need for discrete times for literacy and numeracy but these can occur at various times throughout each day.

- Formal teaching of skills still occurs and these are usually linked to the interests and current investigations of the children.

- The role of the teacher is to scaffold and model for the children, and to extend and promote their interests is an integral part of the WLA.

Chapter 7
Planning and documentation

'It's not what is poured into a student that counts, but what is planted.'

Linda Conway

Introduction

This chapter provides the details and processes for WLA planning. Planning is a critical aspect of the pedagogy. It provides the basis for all teaching and learning and reassures teachers and teams of teachers that while children may at times be working on individual investigations, the key intentions for learning and development are identified regularly and can link directly back into government requirements and frameworks.

The WLA planning process is rigorous and extremely relevant and dynamic, ensuring that teachers are not only planning intentions for learning and development, but are also able to respond to the immediate needs, interests and strengths of children.

The planning process is often referred to as a two-stream approach:

1. The teaching team identify learning and development intentions each fortnight.

2. The teacher responds to the spontaneous moments of learning which emerge from the children during their investigations.

Planning also includes a number of related strategies for the purposes of individual records and observations. They are also included in this chapter.

Principles of the planning process

The WLA is an integrated curriculum; the approach integrates elements of literacy, numeracy and other learning areas (i.e. general studies) together, alongside children's interests. There is no need for separate integrated studies units.

The WLA does not use or advocate topics, focuses or themes in planning. Nor does the WLA use scope and sequence charts. The WLA planning is based in part on children within the classroom. Each year, group dynamics and children's strengths and needs differ, thus, planning cannot be projected into years ahead.

Planning for the WLA is not about having a content-driven focus or some key understandings identified for children to acquire on a particular topic. It seeks to integrate learning into a range of interests and issues that emerge from both the child and the teacher or community.

The WLA philosophy moves teachers away from recipe- and prescription-driven planning to repertoire- and principle-based planning

Planning is based on a continuous cycle of setting intentions, observation and assessment linked to children's interests and skills, and then further planning. The aims of the planning process are:

- to plan for children's stage of maturity, learning and interests first

- to identify intentions for learning in disciplines such as literacy and numeracy

- to link learning intentions and skill instruction sessions directly to age- and stage-appropriate experiences and to the children's interests as much as possible.

Commencement of planning from the identified learning intentions and developmental domain intentions is a re-conceptualisation of the planning process. It requires teachers to consider the children (their development and interests) and the teacher's learning intentions as the first and most important part of any plan.

Planning process cycle

- *Set developmental intentions.*

- *Set learning intentions—based on literacy and numeracy intentions and other subject requirements.*

- *Link intentions to state and national framework outcomes.*

- *Identify children's interests.*

- *Identify additional school or community interests or concepts.*

- *Provide a range of learning experiences and provocations based on interests and intentions which can be used in investigators as well as in formal literacy and numeracy experiences.*

- *Observe children's interests, skills and understandings as they work.*

- *Include assessment processes.*

- *Carry out further planning (based on the above) each fortnight.*

There is constant balance of setting objectives based on two key factors:

- *intentions set by teachers tied to learning intentions*

- *additional and modified objectives once children have been observed.*

This is described as the 'emergent' curriculum—setting the balance between what we want for the children, what we see them demonstrate and how we can respond to them (Stacey 2009).

Terminology used

The terminology and language used in the WLA is reflected in the planning. Goals, intentions or aims (not standards, benchmarks or outcomes) are used in the planning and discussions between staff. This is an important part of the approach. Developmentally, we can hold aims and objectives for children in their development and learning, but we cannot predict that all children will be ready to reach a particular standard or outcome simply based on chronological age.

The plan identifies intentions, but does not state a particular standard or outcome that must be reached within a given time frame. This however, does not mean that intervention, supports and extensions do not occur. Rather, it is when to intervene and the nature of intervention that need to be carefully considered. For example, traditional reading intervention programs that select a particular age or grade level are not required in this approach. Some children may require intervention earlier, some may simply need more time to mature and some may need intervention later.

Curriculum framework learning standards can be used as the learning intentions providing consistency between government requirements and the developmental approach.

Planning stages

Stage one: Developmental domain overviews

A yearly overview of developmental domains is provided for all children across the first three years of school. These developmental domains are based on development and should not be confused with values. Consider the following example:

We wish all children (as they mature and become adults) to develop an ability to cooperate and collaborate with each other.

This is a reasonable value to hold for children, as society needs to reflect a level of cooperation. However, young children have limited empathy and are still working and interacting at an associative or parallel level. Remembering this ensures we do not try to make young children cooperate before they are ready. A better intention might be 'for all children to work and play alongside each other'.

The setting of the developmental domain intentions is the first and most critical part of the planning process. It is what essentially makes the difference between this approach and other approaches to curriculum design and planning. Deficit models are not used in WLA planning. Rather, the approach seeks to identify both needs and strengths of each child to build upon, extend or intervene in—this is a non-deficit model.

The developmental domain intentions are highly specific so that measurement can be undertaken during the teacher's observations. They will also be the basis for the ways in which many of the actual learning experiences are set up. There are a number of books and lists that describe the developmental domains in detail to help teachers in their planning and observation (Allen & Martos

2007; Copple & Bredekamp 2009). Each school is encouraged to construct their own developmental domain overviews, but an example is supplied on the CD.

The following developmental domains need to be considered when setting intentions for the whole group.

Emotional maturity

This is often also known as the affective domain. It refers to children's developing identity, self concept, emotions, expression of needs and attachment. It encompasses the development of the self.

Social

This refers to the self in relation to others, and includes awareness of others, interactions, initiation of contact with others, relationships with others, pro-social skills, interpersonal communication and awareness of diversity.

Language

This refers mostly to oral and communicative language, language expression, verbal expression, speech, articulation, speaking, listening and vocabulary.

Cognitive

This refers to and means thinking skills. Thinking includes problem solving, lateral and creative thought, perspective and sensory awareness, decision making, imaginative thinking, initiative, prediction, memory and recall.

Physical

This refers to gross and fine motor skills, bilateral coordination, spatial awareness, body image and awareness and health.

The wording that frames this part of the documentation is: 'For the children to …' This helps the teacher to explicitly highlight what it is they want for the children's learning. For example, for the children to:

- be introduced to
- consolidate
- demonstrate
- revise
- extend…

Stage two: Setting learning intentions

Fortnightly planning process: The statement of intent (SOI)

Fortnightly intentions for the children are developed from aspects of the yearly overview. Remember that development is a biological maturation process. We can't make children work in a particular way if they are not yet ready. Setting these goals therefore provides a reality check for teachers to maintain appropriate expectations for learning, based on the biological readiness of the children.

Teachers work in teams to plan fortnightly. The overall developmental and learning objectives will be similar between team members and this ensures consistency for auditing purposes across teams. However, the actual learning experiences will differ between classrooms because the children in each class will generate different interests and investigations. This is the essence of providing personalised and responsive learning opportunities for children to engage in meaningful and relevant experiences. Individual needs and strengths of children are also identified through the focus child system, which is described in Chapter 3 and later in this chapter.

One way of thinking about this in most instances, is that the actual experience, investigation or activity is simply a means by which skills, understandings and learning occur. The specific nature of what the project or activity is, should never be the major starting point for planning. For example, the starting point in planning is not, 'We are doing living things next term'. Rather it is, 'What are our intentions for learning and development?' and 'What other issues or focus may we also wish to introduce?'

The fortnightly planner is referred to as a 'statement of intent' (SOI). While teachers plan ahead and ensure they know the needs and learning intentions for children, the SOI sets out an intention of how they wish to proceed. It is also flexible enough to be responsive to the children's particular needs, skills or interests as they arise. It is recommended that the SOI is completed electronically so that teachers can 'cut and paste' each fortnight into the next SOI for evaluation and planning. Table 7.1 provides an example of a completed SOI and a pro forma is on the CD.

Learning intentions can be taken from the government or school's existing curriculum documentation, but they should be identified as intentions rather than standards. These intentions are the full list of major foci in key learning areas for the fortnight. It is not necessary to keep a separate list of learning intentions. The wording here always emphasises 'For the children to:

- consolidate
- extend
- revise
- revise
- recognise
- explore
- investigate
- develop…'

Examples of learning objectives

Maths

- For the children to develop 1:1 correspondence

English

- For the children to recognise sounds
- For the children to explore procedural text

Science

- For the children to investigate the properties of magnets

Stage three: Identifying children's interests

These are things that children have shown an interest in; things teachers might predict they will be interested in; or things that at this stage in their lives and within a particular community, teachers know they have an interest in. Children may also have demonstrated some of the interests through their investigation time (however it is not limited to only what the teacher observes during investigations).

Teachers brainstorm the range of interests that the children currently reflect. These are used as the basis for some of the actual learning instruction and investigation experiences that will be promoted during the next fortnight.

The teacher may have noticed that some of the children were making a pizza shop in the dramatic play area. In linking to literacy and numeracy, children may be encouraged or expected to make menus, provide prices, write a specials board, take orders from others or work the cash register.

Stage four: Teacher, school and community interests

Teacher, school and community interests are elements that are also used as part of the planning stage. Some schools may reflect particular religious festivals or local community events. These can be integrated into and alongside the rich range of other experiences that are provided. The school may also identify particular concepts or values that they wish to incorporate.

Community interests are added in as intentions at this stage. For example, the language used is not, 'We are doing sustainability', but rather, considering the stage of development and understanding of children in the early years, the intention might read, 'For the children to take responsibility for recycling their materials, lunch scraps and litter.' Specifying community interests with an intention before the actual focus or content helps to ensure that the learning is developmentally appropriate and not just about values of a particular community. Remember that due to the egocentric nature of children's brain

Table 7.1 Completed statement of intent

Statement of intent
Preschool–Grade 2

Developmental domain objectives	Learning objectives	Children's current interests	Staff/school/community interests	Learning experiences	Modifications
Emotional For the children to: • continue to self-initiate choices • follow through with decisions • verbalise their feelings in relation to anger, sadness, happiness **Social** For the children to: • work and play alongside others in the space appropriately • grow in awareness of others' needs and perspectives, including teachers **Language** For the children to: • listen, attend and follow directions • identify sounds in the middle of words • use correct sentence structure and punctuation **Cognitive** For the children to: • describe aspects of their learning to their peers • reflect on their investigations and make future plans • understand the relationship between cause and effect **Physical** For the children to: • refine their mature tripod grip so they can hold a pencil appropriately • refine their spatial awareness in order to move around the room	**English** For the children to: • recognise 'ed' as a phonogram for showing past tense in some words • recognise 'oi', 'oy', 'ai', 'ay', 'ea' and the most common words using these phonograms • use capital letters and full stops in their writing • recognise that cards and letters are a form of communication and write their own to send **Maths** For the children to: • recognise and name 3D shapes • model place value of whole numbers • skip count by 2s, 5s and 10s • answer doubles and near-doubles number facts	• Museums • Dinosaurs • Bugs • Christmas • Paper-making • Cooking • Cities and buildings • Magnets	• Christmas • Graduation ceremony • Sustaining the environment • Recycling • Visitors to the classroom	**Interest Areas** • Magnets • Gumnuts • Christmas around the world **Dramatic Play** • Junior Masterchef kitchen • Home corner • North Pole tray **Reading** • Book area, including texts about Christmas, recycling, cooking **Construction** • Making table with cellophane, Christmas paper • Blocks, with farm and zoo animals • Lego technic • Multi-link (outdoors) **Sensory** • Salt dough • Snow • Water tub • Shaving cream • Sand tray • Paper making **Writing** • Message boards • Writing tables • Card making **Maths** • IWB number chart • 3D shapes • Cooking **Art** • Painting easel • Natural collage easel • Sewing **Fine Motor** • Threading • Tweezers and marbles	

maturity, attempting to get them to appreciate or understand the worldwide implications of sustainability is inappropriate. Starting with the immediate world of young children is more meaningful and relevant to their own lives. Starting with an intention also helps the teacher to focus on the skill or understanding to be developed.

> Instead of thinking 'we will make a vegetable garden' as a topic, consider what intentions you have in mind that may lead to one of the projects including a vegetable garden, but not limit the thinking to just the garden as the focus. For example, the intention may be for the children to be exposed to concepts of growth, nurturing and sustainability.

This way of thinking also helps to build inclusive approaches to community events and to children and families of culturally diverse backgrounds, with a range of family structures, and with a range of interests and needs.

Instead of thinking of 'doing a project on family', the intentions might include, 'To promote thinking about people who are important in our lives', to help children identify people significant to them. One of the ways of meeting this intention may be to discuss family types, but there is also a wider range of strategies and ideas that can be used in order to meet these intentions. This broadens the scope of the discussion and helps to engage children who will also identify their own interpretations and experiences.

Stage five: Identifying learning experiences, materials and resources that can help children meet objectives through active engagement

This is finally where the teacher plans the actual learning experiences—in a child-centred pedagogy the teacher can only plan the learning experiences once they have the knowledge and understanding gained through the completion of the prior four stages. In traditional teaching, the planning often starts at stage five ('What are we doing?') rather than at stage one ('What do we want for the children?').

Stage five involves planning for the children during the following fortnight. The planning includes all aspects of the day and week: investigations and formal teaching (whole group and small group). All the specific information on intentions and details for literacy, numeracy and the types of groups can be contained in this section of the plan.

The actual experiences should attempt to include developmental and learning intentions together. Setting up a range of activities (dramatic play, blocks and constructions) and provocations which reflect the interests of the children provides many opportunities for them to experience some of the intentions the teacher may have set.

Developmental domain objectives

- For the children to work in parallel alongside each other

- For the children to express their own views and ideas

Learning objectives

- For the children to classify and recognise shapes

- For the children to recognise the sound of 'd'

Some of the children may be interested in dinosaurs. The teacher may set up two or three different dinosaur play areas—one in the block area, another in a small cosy corner and another in some sand or mud in a water trough.

The children may engage in that play alongside each other; they may be asked to group the dinosaurs and report back to a group or the whole class.

The investigation is directed to varying degrees by the teacher, depending on intentions. It is important to note that it is not necessary or practical to provide different and individual experiences for every child in the class. Personalising the work and learning is based on the nature of and range of investigations which allow individual children to explore in many ways that are meaningful to them, rather than having separate work for each child.

Stage six: The adult role

This part of the plan helps to focus the teacher on what specific areas or major strategies they will be working on. It may include specific language, ideas to model or instruction strategies that will be a prompt for the teacher. It can also be useful for parent helpers, additional staff and relief teachers (see relief teacher information sheet on the CD) in understanding some of the goals for learning.

Stage seven: Modifications and additions

The WLA is a responsive pedagogy framed by learning and developmental teaching intentions thus the teaching must be flexible and dynamic. The modifications and additions provide this flexibility and dynamism by adding, deleting, changing and modifying some of the experiences and to capture some of these on the planning document. The planning has been developed to be dynamic, responsive and open to change.

Recording and documenting the learning

One of the key aspects of the WLA is to capture on a regular basis the learning and developmental needs and strengths of each child. This helps the teacher to personalise the learning and to be increasingly responsive to each child's particular interests and needs or strengths as much as is practicable.

Individual record sheet

Meaningful development and learning does not occur in quick bursts of a day or even a week. Understandings, experiences, skills, development and learning continue to occur, and are often revisited, refined, extended and consolidated over time. One of the key strategies for setting appropriate individual goals for children is to use the focus child system. In this system each child will have an electronic file where the teacher makes notes on development, key learning areas and key framework outcomes. The teacher records daily on each of the focus children and any other children who have done something the teacher wants to document. This should take not more than 10 to 15 minutes per day and provides an authentic, meaningful and continual record of the children's development and learning. Table 7.2 is an example of the individual record sheet and a pro forma is on the CD.

Other forms of documenting and capturing children's interests and learning

Daily record sheet

During investigation times each day, a one-page overview of children's investigations and ideas can be jotted down so that the teacher has an immediate record of what the children are engaged in. This helps to plan, direct and scaffold the children the following day or later in the same day. This is considered the teacher's memory jogger—the opportunity to jot down ideas quickly and easily without having to hold everything in their heads. A template is provided on the CD.

Photographs

Children love to see themselves at work. Photographs are a useful and integral part of the WLA. Photos can be used to reflect with children by watching a slide show at the end of each day or the commencement of the next day to help tune the children into the learning. Photos may be placed into a hard copy handout for children to look through, write about, or take notes on. The teacher may use photographs to help parents not only see what their child was working on, or who they were working with, but also what learning was actually taking place. Children can also use photographs to make books of their own, or of class work to be used as part of literacy activities.

Portfolios of children's learning

Children are encouraged to collect their own examples of their learning and investigations. Ensuring each child has a scrapbook for their design briefs—it means that these can be stored in one location rather than as numerous scraps of paper. Children can also use these scrapbooks for reflection on learning and future planning with teachers and parents.

Displays of children's investigations which describe the learning and skills (not just the activity) are important and can also help with parent information and education.

All of these forms of documentation not only support and document children's learning and interests and help in the planning cycle, but also provide a rich and broad range of assessment tools. Assessment is described in more detail in Chapter 8.

Table 7.2 Individual record sheet

the Walker Learning Approach DEVELOPMENTALLY APPROPRIATE PRACTICE	**Individual record**
Child's name Julie Smith	**Date of birth** 29/09/07

Development	
Social	25/3 Julie is initiating contact and discussion with a range of peers. 4/4 Julie tends to dominate the social interactions.
Emotional	25/3 Julie is having trouble expressing her frustrations verbally with her peers. 6/4 Julie is currently unsettled and easily upset. Her father is away overseas.
Cognitive	27/3 Julie often reflects lateral thinking and good problem-solving.
Language	4/4 Julie uses appropriate grammar in tenses when describing events.
Physical	25/3 Julie's general upper body coordination seems appropriate, with good strength in arms when swinging on the monkey bars.
Developmental objective	Focus for Term 1: For Julie to extend her positive initiation with peers but to also learn how to express her feelings and frustrations with her peers

Key learning areas	
Literacy observation	25/3 Julie is recognising key words and aspects of punctuation including full stops, question marks. 7/4 Julie enjoys reading and choosing her own books.

Table 7.2 continued next page

Table 7.2 Individual record sheet (continued)

Literacy goal	For Julie to use expression in her words and continue to sound out when reading.
Numeracy observation	25/3 Julie is demonstrating appropriate basic number skills and understandings. Seems to particularly enjoy numeracy classes.
Numeracy goal	For Julie to be extended in her number understanding and commence more complex addition.
Key framework outcomes (Victorian example)	
Community	25/3 Julie mixes with her peers and has a sense of the school community.
Communication	25/3 As above in language: proficient but needs support with personal expression.
Identity	14/4 Julie has a strong sense of her place in her family and her Vietnamese culture and language.
Wellbeing	13/4 Julie seems settled, physically well and strong and emotionally secure.
Specific interests/topics	Julie particularly loves TV shows (especially High Five) Julie participated in ballet and singing in Term 1
Additional information	Julie's father absent for a month due to work overseas. This was unsettling for her.
Parent comment	Good to hear she has started her year and term so positively. Good to get feedback on her missing Dad. We noticed it at home too.

Summary

- Planning is done fortnightly with the teaching team together using the statement of intent (SOI)

- Planning commences with developmental intentions and then learning intentions. Each fortnight these are checked against state/territory outcomes.

- Pre-planned term topics are not used in any way as planning is based on developmental and learning intentions.

- Learning experiences and activities are based both on the authentic interests of the child, what happens in investigations plus teachers' ideas and interests and events.

- Overall goals for learning and development are set on a yearly basis (usually based on a government framework) but broken down to reflect time of year, development of children and strengths and interests of the children.

- Planning is carried out fortnightly and is dynamic and constantly responsive to the children's interest and engagement.

- Linking group plans to individual children is reflected through the individual observation record.

- A range of documentation to collect examples of learning and projects is used to continue the planning cycle and to help scaffold children and extend their learning and interests.

- Photographs, scrapbooks, portfolios and journals are all ways in which children can reflect and collate authentic samples of their work.

Chapter 8
Assessment and reporting

'Not everything that counts can be counted and not everything that can be counted counts.'

Albert Einstein

Introduction

This chapter is in two sections. The first section discusses the principles of assessment and provides practical examples of the range of strategies that can be used for assessment, observation and monitoring children's learning within the WLA.

The second section of the chapter considers a range of strategies used in the WLA for sharing and reporting children's learning and development with parents.

Benchmarks and standards

On first implementing the WLA, a common question from teachers is, 'But what about benchmarks and standards?' This question reflects the current pressure that many teachers are under to move their children to particular standards as set by government expectations. The reality is of course that children can't necessarily reach benchmarks just because a government says they should. This question also reflects a belief or fear that perhaps children who are playing and working on investigations as in the WLA will be even more unlikely to achieve the required standards. Nothing could be further from the truth.

The WLA is a rigorous curriculum that immerses children in rich and meaningful learning experiences whereby the children are experiencing more oral language, more writing about their tasks and more numeracy embedded into their investigations than in the traditional classroom. In addition, teachers are scaffolding and using formal teaching instruction through clinic groups and whole group discussions to promote and instruct particular skills along the way. Our own research and data collected from schools over the past 15 years has shown unequivocally that children's learning in all key outcomes including literacy and numeracy is enhanced significantly (Walker 2009).

The interests of children are one of the major tools that teachers can use when instructing and providing formal skills sessions. International research indicates strongly that rather than lessening skills and learning, pedagogies based on the same philosophy as the WLA actually enhance children's learning, increase their levels of engagement, reduce behavioural disturbance and sustain reading levels and writing skills throughout their primary and secondary years (Marcon 2003).

It is reassuring to know that children's learning can be enhanced through the WLA, and also that their social and emotional development is improved. It is true however, that some children within the classroom will not reach the expected government standards, regardless of whether they are in a developmental or a traditional classroom. They may have additional learning challenges, or simply they may not be ready.

This is where the issue of holding a philosophical belief about teaching and learning is paramount. The reality about child development is that not all children will be ready to learn at the same time. Some children require longer to attain the maturity that assists them with their learning. Teachers may know that a child is just not ready, but the government expects a particular standard. This tension can be eased through leadership and commitment to a child-centred curriculum. Classroom teachers can feel less stressed if their leadership recognises that some children will require longer time to attain particular benchmarks, and that the children who do not reach the standards are not reflecting poor teaching practice.

Schools that use the WLA are still working within the expectations and requirements of government. However, the WLA places the realities of the children first and then makes the system work around those realities, rather than being driven by external expectations. The WLA would never state, 'All children must be at this reading level by the end of their first year.' Rather, the WLA would assert, 'Let us aim for these particular goals and to move each child further along their own learning process.'

While we might have a goal to move children along the continuum of learning in reading and writing, there is no pressure or expectation that all children must get there within the same timeframe.

Assessment within the WLA, therefore, considers a wide range of factors for each individual child. Goals are still set, the state or national curriculum can still be used, but the range of assessment techniques highlights that the child is not just reaching a reading level, but attaining skills in a range of areas.

There is no doubt that current reporting systems which attempt to lock children into grade levels and progression points run in direct opposition to the philosophy of the WLA. However, this chapter provides some examples of how schools are attempting to work within the expectations (while placing the child at the centre of the curriculum), rather than expecting things of students that they may not be ready for.

Assessment as opposed to testing

Assessment actually means monitoring and evaluating in order to move forward.

> *The greatest and most meaningful question a teacher or parent can consider about learning is not, 'Where is this child in relation to the rest of the class or the state or the country?' but rather, 'Where was this child, where are they now and where are they headed?'*

Defined in this way, assessment provides some important ideas for focus within the WLA classroom. We wish to know where children currently are in relation to their development, prior experiences, understandings and academic skills. Once we have observed, documented and monitored each child individually, we can better plan and implement further learning opportunities based on their strengths as well as the areas of learning they cannot yet achieve.

> *This is one of the important aspects of the WLA. It is concerned with extending children from their strengths and does not use a 'deficit' model whereby children are only viewed or assessed in relation to what they cannot do.*

Standardised testing

Assessment is different from testing. Standardised testing is not part of the philosophy of the WLA. The philosophy of the WLA rejects the notion that useful information for children and teachers can be ascertained though a standardised test set on a particular day at a particular time for all children. The great diversity in how children express their learning and understanding and the differences between children in relation to language, culture and learning cannot be represented meaningfully or realistically through a standardised test.

In schools or states where standardised testing is mandated, the WLA encourages schools to actively provide information to parents about the greater range of meaningful assessment tools that are used, so that parents understand the limitations of standardised testing. The WLA is opposed to and advocates against teachers 'teaching to the test', or for teachers to feel driven to instruct children on how to do the test and to practise tests. Testing through formalised standardised tests is not part of the WLA philosophy.

Entry tests in the first year

There are always some limitations to tests administered by teachers individually to children in their first weeks of Term 1. Children are still forming relationships with teachers and getting used to a new environment, routines and expectations. They are unlikely to give an accurate and meaningful set of answers to the questions about colour, shape or other questions. In fact, many children are overcome by these questions and do not give a response that reflects their knowledge.

Many teachers use this time at the beginning of the year for forming relationships with children and getting to know them through chatting. Teachers' direct observation of children during their first month of working on investigations will provide a more accurate reflection of children's understandings of those basic concepts and also give a much richer range of information to teachers about their current interests, strengths, skills and knowledge than a standardised test. While entry testing may initially serve a limited purpose as a starting point, we find that direct observation of children in their learning provides a more comprehensive view of the child.

Assessment strategies

The WLA assessment encompasses a range of strategies that many classroom teachers are already using.

Reflection strategies

One of the most meaningful opportunities we can model and provide for children as the major tool in learning is to reflect on their own learning, understanding and skills rather than simply being judged and assessed by others.

Provide times for children to reflect on their morning session, the investigations they have made and have been involved in. Teachers can ask questions such as:

- 'What were you learning about or discovering through your investigation?'
- 'What was challenging or hard?'
- 'What might you do next?'
- 'Let's think about some of the reading and writing you needed in that project.'

Reflection can occur when children are working in small groups or individually and the teacher asks questions of the child in order to help them articulate their learning.

Self assessment and reflection

This is where children are actively encouraged to write about or talk about their learning and the things they find easy, challenging or interesting. Sometimes they like to do this by speaking into a voice recorder or by creating a book of photos and samples of their own work.

Peer assessment and reflection

Children can reflect and share with each other about the skills and interests they observe in each other. This often occurs naturally in the WLA as children are often sharing information, discussing and allocating each other to roles and responsibilities.

Portfolios

Portfolios do not need to be a time-consuming project for teachers each term. Meaningful portfolios reflect an authentic snapshot of children's learning, investigations, literacy and numeracy as well as their social and emotional development.

The portfolios are collated during each term by the children and teachers, therefore avoiding a huge rush toward the end of the term.

The portfolio, while a great tool for sharing information with parents, is actually part of the ongoing assessment, evaluation and reflection for children in their learning. With the teacher, children share the responsibility for collecting and collating the portfolio. It is viewed as a real and dynamic assessment tool and often shared between children.

Diagnostic assessment

From time to time, teachers may wish to observe or find out more about children. There are a number of diagnostic tools for assessing children's social skills as well as their thinking, literacy and numeracy.

Small group assessment

Through discussion, small group assessment helps the teacher to identify understandings children have of particular skills. The impromptu comments children make such as 'First I put that one on the top and the round window on the bottom' give teachers an indication of the concepts that the children already know or don't know.

> *Meaningful assessment is used as an indication to the teacher, student and parent of where the child is currently and what skills or understandings need to be planned for in the future. Observation is a key to meaningful assessment in the WLA.*

In the early years of school, assessment is also about observing the children's written reports and design briefs in their projects, in order to identify what skills and needs the teacher can scaffold and extend. Formal testing with worksheets is not necessary.

Running records, listening to children reading and collecting samples of their handwriting are all parts of meaningful assessment which help teachers to know where each child is in relation to their skill acquisition, needs, strengths and future learning.

Tracking children twice each term through in-depth observation is part of the planning and assessment cycle. This happens when each child (along with two other children) is a focus child during a week. The role of the focus children is described in detail in Chapters 3 and 6.

Reporting strategies

The aim of reporting is to help children, parents and teachers share an understanding of the learning, development, attitudes and behaviours that are developing as the child moves through their learning each year. Contrary to general public views or government expectations, meaningful reporting is not about attempting to grade or place a child at a level in comparison with everyone else twice a year.

Sharing information from and with parents

> *The WLA philosophy regards each child's individual learning as the most important information to be shared between the family and the school. Importantly, the children should be a major part of the reporting process and that reporting needs to occur in a variety of ways throughout each year.*

Parent/teacher/student meetings

Traditionally, parent teacher interviews were held without the child being present. The WLA believes that the child's voice, input and presence is vital to a meaningful discussion. A child's learning should not be a secret, nor should meaningful discussion occur without the child. Children as young as preschool age can participate in these interviews. Children can share or talk about their portfolio, chat to the teacher and parents for a few minutes about their learning and listen to the teacher and parents discussing the learning. If there is a significant issue that the teacher or parent does not wish to share in front of the child, this conversation needs to occur at another time and does not have to wait for the interview.

Formal information sessions

These provide the school or teacher with the opportunity to share significant information or issues with parents about teaching and learning. For example, some schools use these information sessions as a way of describing the format of the school report—which parts reflect the WLA and which parts are mandated by the government.

Conversations

These are a more informal way in which the school or teacher can report to parents by sharing information about the curriculum, the WLA and the sorts of learning and intentions that are being worked on and targeted at any particular time. These sessions are sometimes known as conversations with parents and staff. They are less formal than an actual presentation and often teachers and parents sit together in a circle to discuss, ask questions and get to know each other a little more. In some schools, children are also present at these.

Notices outside classrooms

Placing examples of the learning and development intentions outside the classroom each fortnight and displaying the children's work helps parents to see what learning and experiences are occurring on a regular basis. Many schools use portfolios with captions to indicate where the learning and skills are found through the investigations.

Report forms

Most states require a formal written report to be given to parents at least twice a year. Schools use a variety of different strategies and formats to do this. Some states now have a mandated report form, although it is worth noting that schools can request an exemption from these if they provide supporting information on the range and type of reporting that is given to parents.

The WLA views the report as sitting alongside all other types of reporting and information provided to children and parents throughout each year. The report is viewed as one minor part of the reporting process and most often uses descriptive comments on both the development of the child as well as their interest, literacy, numeracy and other learning areas.

Where reports are mandated, the WLA suggests placing a one-page descriptive summary of child development and learning on the front page to highlight that the most important part of the report is neither the grading nor the level. We recommend using the individual observation record as the descriptive summary to share examples of each child's individual journey over the course of the year.

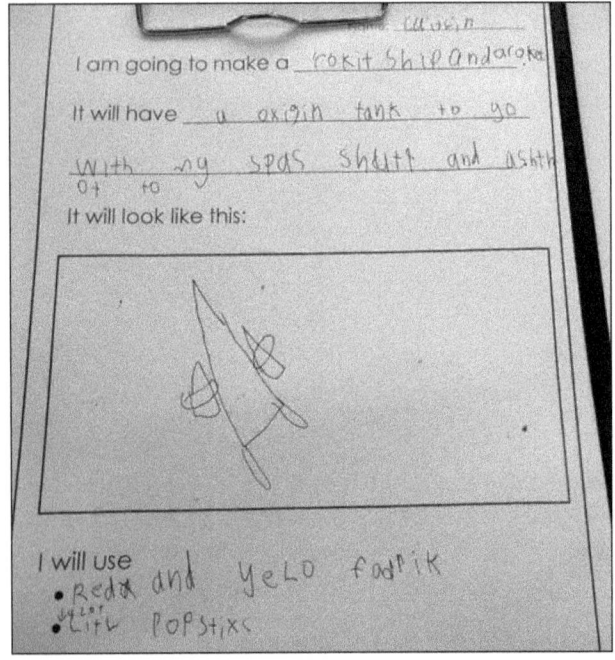

Figure 8.1 Written reports

In the early years of school, assessment is also about observing the children's written reports and design briefs in their projects, in order to identify what skills and needs the teacher can scaffold and extend. Formal testing with worksheets is not necessary.

Summary

- Assessment in the WLA is used to monitor and to help teachers and children plan to extend and support children's learning.

- Assessment is not used to test children in order to rank or grade them in relation to the rest of the class.

- Observation is one of the major tools for meaningful assessment in the WLA.

- Self assessment/reflection and peer assessment/reflection are integral parts of the assessment process.

- Children, parents and teachers should share information together at sessions such as parent/teacher/student interviews.

- Written reports are presented to parents as descriptive summaries, rather than as gradings or rankings of children.

- Reporting to parents uses a range of strategies and the formal written report is one of the least important parts of the process.

Chapter 9

Embedding child development, literacy and numeracy intentions

'The only person who is educated is the one who has learned how to learn and change.'

Carl Rogers

Introduction

In the WLA, literacy and numeracy are integrated into many different parts of the day—sometimes embedded within the children's investigation, and at other times formally instructed by the teacher. This chapter presents a range of strategies that are used within the WLA to help facilitate literacy and numeracy.

The philosophy of the WLA is based on the belief that learning occurs through a range of integrated experiences which are active, hands-on, creative and open-ended. These personalised investigative play-based experiences are planned for the children and are rich and meaningful and promote sustained literacy, numeracy and language development.

In recent years, most specific programs (such as the Victorian Department of Education Early Years Literacy Block) used across Australia have usually timetabled literacy and numeracy into discrete two-hour blocks of time dominated by rotations of activities for children. Many of the strategies found within specific literacy or numeracy programs are useful and the WLA still embraces formal instruction—some discrete instruction on guided reading, handwriting, exploration of mathematical concepts, number and time is still required. In the WLA, however, the nature of when, how and in what context this instruction is given differs slightly from more traditional concepts of literacy or numeracy blocks.

Rotations of short duration or many rotations during one session are not part of this approach. The WLA recognises that in the early years, children need time to engage in meaningful experiences; time to perhaps move away and then time to return to the experience. The WLA does not wish to place strict time restrictions on children for their learning to occur. The WLA also acknowledges that literacy and numeracy are embedded within all life experiences.

Literacy and numeracy are still taught explicity in discrete sessions throughout the week in WLA classrooms. Literacy and numeracy are also embedded in cross-curricula learning, play and investigations.

Principles of literacy and numeracy within the WLA

- Literacy and numeracy are often embedded into other learning experiences such as SOSE and not necessarily viewed as discrete or separate learning areas.

- The content areas of the curriculum (SOSE, science, health) are used to develop children's literacy and numeracy skills.

- Formal teaching and instruction through clinic and whole groups is still used, but can be at various times throughout the day.

- The skill of the WLA teacher is to utilise children's interests, skills and current knowledge as the catalysts for building on and introducing meaningful and relevant explicit instruction.

- Formal literacy and numeracy instruction attempts to link the skills being taught directly to the interests and investigations of the children to help promote meaningful links for the child.

- Literacy and numeracy must be embedded within a range of investigative play-based experiences that make explicit links back to the purposes of literacy and numeracy within everyday life.

- Literacy and numeracy experiences are found in many opportunities and experiences including outdoor learning.

- Numeracy involves the range of skills that reflect being able to represent, classify and understand number, spatial relations and time within meaningful contexts.

- Goals of language and literacy are for children to expand their ability to communicate through speaking, listening, reading and writing.

- Technical skills or sub-skills, such as word recognition, punctuation, handwriting and letter formation, are taught in a range of ways that are meaningful to children.

Literacy

- Literacy and children's play are both symbolic and integrally paired.

- Literacy reflects and conveys meaning and representation within children's play.

- Literacy and language are part of everyday life experiences.

- Investigations that are enriched with literacy provide opportunities for children to make connections to their everyday life experiences.

- Literacy within play scaffolds children's learning where they can explore a range of functions and features of literacy.

Examples of embedding rich literacy intentions in the WLA

Literacy includes the need for a range of learning experiences such as:

- *opportunities to symbolically express thoughts and ideas*

- *rich oral language experiences and discussions through dramatic play and role play*

- *extending creative expression and ideas into written representation*

- *reading from books that are created through investigations*

- *talking personally and meaningfully with others*

- *expressing feelings in words*

- *describing attributes*

- *reading, being read to or listening to stories, rhymes and language through listening posts (including high quality literature and non-fiction for pleasure and research)*

- *writing about experiences*

- *planning and implementing projects*

- *listing requirements*

- *making books that may reflect narrative, reports or procedures from investigations*

- *recording voices and language*

- *making signs to be used in investigations*

- *creating menus, instructions, diagrams*

- *design briefs and maps (used to help a child plan and design their investigation before they commence construction)*

- *procedural texts based on children's own constructions and creations*

- *sounds and letter recognition based on children's investigations as well as directed or introduced by the teacher*

- *creating lists for various tasks children may be engaged in during their projects and investigations*

- *following plans with the teacher on a whiteboard each morning as children reflect and organise their day*

- *children signing themselves in instead of the teacher reading out names at roll call*

- *children signing themselves out when they go to work outside*

- *thought or question of the day (children are invited to share a thought or ask a question that is listed on a board for others to think about and respond to later in the day)*

- *noticeboard to record ideas or special events*

- *notices for parents written by children*

- *homemade individual spelling books*

- *common words on walls around room.*

Numeracy

In almost all experiences it is possible to use aspects of numeracy in children's investigations as part of everyday life.

> **Examples of embedding rich numeracy intentions in the WLA**
>
> Many aspects of real life experiences promote numeracy. Key elements of numeracy include:
>
> - *experiencing and representing*
> - *classification*
> - *seriation*
> - *number*
> - *time*
> - *spatial relations*
> - *shapes and colour*
> - *relative portions*
>
> These can be introduced through learning experiences such as:
>
> - *recognising objects, touch, smell, taste*
> - *imitating actions and sounds*
> - *relating models, photographs and pictures to real situations*
> - *investigating and describing objects*
> - *using objects in different ways*
> - *talking about characteristics, similarities and differences in order to distinguish and make comparisons*
> - *holding more than one attribute in mind at a time*
> - *ordering, arranging, counting and rearranging*
> - *comparing amounts*
> - *fitting things together and taking them apart*
> - *using a woodwork bench (for hammering, counting nails, designing, measuring lengths of wood)*
> - *block buildings (for height and positional language experiences)*
> - *collecting and representing information (such as colours of teacher's cars)*
> - *dramatic play (cost of food on a menu, using a cash register, counting money, profit and loss in a shop).*

Incorporating literacy, numeracy and other skills in the WLA classroom

There are many opportunities for children to be immersed in literacy, language and numeracy within the learning environment. These are planned for within the investigations of the children and the teacher will scaffold opportunities to extend literacy and numeracy through these opportunities.

Children also need to be involved in metacognitive and multi-literacy skills. They need to think about their thinking and to recognise different elements of thought such as lateral, reflective, evaluative, creative and perspective. Through active, hands-on investigations, children are planning, predicting, scheming, reflecting and discussing with each other, which facilitates metacognition. For example, when faced with wishing to create a shop, doctor's surgery or veterinary clinic in their dramatic play, children are immersed in endless possibilities for literacy and thinking to be used, modelled and taught.

> **WLA dramatic play example:**
> **Fish and chip shop**
>
> In the shop, children wanted to have a specials board, a TV (that had to have a remote control designed and built so customers could watch the TV while waiting for their order), a menu, a writing pad to take orders, a chef who had to have recipes to follow to make the food, placemats with the name of the shop on them,

> a map of how to find the shop, and an entry in the phone book so people could ring and place orders.
>
> Through the teachers' scaffolding, prompting and following these ideas of the children, a range of literacy, numeracy and metacognitive skills was demonstrated, practised and then later reinforced through clinic and whole group discussions.

Consider the range of literacy skills in the above example:

- speaking
- listening
- writing
- reading
- letter formation
- capitals
- spelling
- listing
- sentence construction

A number of numeracy skills are also involved:

- the food has to be paid for
- money has to be exchanged
- a cash register with numbers is used
- the shop owner has to count how much money is in the till each day before trading commences
- some children made credit cards and attempted to work out how much credit they would have left, depending on the amount on the card and the cost of the food
- signs are made with the cost of the food on the menus
- phone numbers are made and written for orders
- timelines are set for how long the food will take to cook
- amounts of food are divided up and cut up for customers.

The WLA therefore, uses children's investigations and ideas to build on, introduce or extend children's literacy and numeracy skills.

The WLA can help with engaging children and it often encourages those who are reluctant to formally write, or find reading a challenge, to simply having fun reading and writing. The need to research books and read about their investigations is a rich, relevant and authentic way to embed literacy into the everyday lives of children and their motivation and levels of engagement are improved through writing about their investigations, or wanting to use a variety of genres (e.g. to assist them in writing a play).

> In one classroom, a preschool child was reluctant to write and appeared anxious to try. The teacher suggested she might like to be a reporter for the morning and with a clipboard move around the room and write down what she could see the children were working on.
>
> Toward the end of the session, the girl had written a whole page of letters, including her own name—which the teacher said she had never done before.
>
> In most cases, linking some of the skills through investigations helps to interest and motivate children, so that when a formal instruction session occurs, they are more interested and less anxious about it. Something almost magical occurs when children are provided with clipboards!

The WLA also reflects that literacy and numeracy do not need to follow a strict order such as a letter or number a week. As long as all letters and basic numerical concepts are introduced, linked to meaningful experiences and embedded within the children's learning and projects, these skills will be acquired. An audit of the letters and concepts introduced and revisited is kept by the teacher to ensure that all sounds and numbers are worked through during the year.

Catching the moment of opportunity is an important feature of the approach linked with literacy and numeracy.

> A teacher in a Grade 1 class noticed that some of the children had created a beach in the sand tray and were sorting and grouping some shells. They were making up nonsense words with the sound 'sh'. She decided to model that sound and letters and the children wrote a 'sh' poem together with the teacher in a clinic group.
>
> The teacher had not planned to introduce this learning at that time; however, the children were developmentally ready, interested, engaged and it was a prime opportunity to scaffold at that point.

Literacy and numeracy however, are not just introduced or scaffolded as a result of the children's interests. The planning process, as described in Chapter 7, shows how the intentions for literacy and numeracy learning each fortnight are clearly and proactively defined and set so that teachers will have clarity about what skills they will focus on for formal instruction groups. Teachers must identify the key literacy and numeracy learning intentions for children before the experiences are introduced. Literacy and numeracy instruction therefore involves two processes usually occurring at the same time.

Teachers have planned for particular intentions and skills to be introduced or consolidated for the coming fortnight. Some of these will be deliberately embedded into the investigations so that the children may have to utilise some of these skills. At the same time, formal skill instruction is planned to assist and model for the children the particular skills set for the fortnight. These instruction times will attempt to use some of the children's investigations at the point of instructing to engage and capture the children's interest. Observing the interests and investigations of the children can be a great leaping-off point (or springboard) from which to introduce a formal instruction session.

While this is occurring, spontaneous elements of literacy and numeracy will also be generated during the children's interactions and investigations. Through observing some of these each day, the teacher can use spontaneous moments to scaffold or introduce a particular skill, even if it wasn't planned.

Even if only one group or one child demonstrated a particular skill, teachers can use this during the reflection time as a way of demonstrating a skill to all of the children. Children are usually very interested in what the others have been working on.

Key organisational factors in establishing a rich WLA literacy and numeracy curriculum

Space in the classroom and outdoors

As described in Chapter 5, both the classroom and outdoor space are important in helping to promote time and opportunity for children to engage in and follow through with their investigations. Promoting literacy and numeracy requires space for posters or prints around the room, as well as space to engage in a variety of investigations linking back to writing, drawing, oral language experiences and documenting work through photographs and journals, measuring, predicting, sorting and classifying.

Dividing and containing spaces as discussed in Chapter 5 provides clear directions to the children on the types of play and literacy or numeracy that can be accessed, and helps to establish patterns and routines where children recognise and can take responsibility for documenting many of their own investigations. Ensuring noticeboards and whiteboards are at child height is part of the way the room is divided and helps to model text and numbers around the room.

Learning outdoors must also accommodate opportunities for children's investigations to be enhanced or enriched by literacy or numeracy. Easels (available for planning or design briefs before the block constructions commence), scrapbooks or paper (for plans and lists) are all required outdoors.

Time

Children require lengthy periods of time to work and engage in their learning. Children pass through a number of key stages in their learning and investigations:

- consideration and choice
- establishing what they wish to select or work on
- planning how
- engaging
- working and thinking
- resting, taking time out
- following through, replenishing
- reflection
- completion.

These processes take time (sometimes days—most often more than one hour). Some children will progress through these stages more quickly than others, depending on what the learning and investigation is about and how the teacher scaffolds and extends the child.

It also helps to place a clock at child level so children can become familiar with reading it.

Practical resources and materials needed in the learning environment

Ensuring a range of open-ended, paper, boxes, dramatic play and construction materials are always available is an important part of literacy and numeracy in this approach. Access to books, computers and research tools is also important.

These resources and equipment provide proactive and explicit opportunities to promote literacy and numeracy as natural parts of the investigations of the children, both inside and outside the classroom, and children become used to accessing them as resources to help with their learning.

Clipboards

As stated previously, something magical happens when early years children are given a clipboard! They seem to think they are important and grown up and are often more highly motivated to write, plan and use these in their investigations. Clipboards can be used in a variety of ways:

- as a reporter
- to take notes on procedures in a dramatic play or construction area
- as menus
- for lists
- for designs, maps and plans.

It is useful to place a neat pile of clipboards in the writer's workshop area, so that children can self-select when and if they need them. It is also useful to place some in strategic areas inside and outside the classroom, for example, in the dramatic play area, near the block or Lego constructions, or near the sensory area of clay or playdough.

Clipboards can be used at reflection time, with children referring to them at the end of the session and teachers using them to model, scaffold or extend a concept or skill.

Scrapbooks or work books

Instead of separate work books for different subjects, we recommend simply using one scrapbook each term for all the learning that occurs, including investigations. This is up to individual teams to decide. One of the benefits that teachers report about keeping all work together is that it is easier for the children to manage one book as opposed to three or four and in addition, it symbolically reinforces that whether the learning occurred in investigations, literacy or numeracy, it is all important and it is all learning. Scrapbooks also facilitate the opportunity for the children to be multi-literate and multi-numerate.

Each child has a scrapbook in which they can record some of their design briefs, thoughts, plans and maps. Having them contained within a book provides the chance to reflect, go back, discuss and describe from experiences in the past. The scrapbook presents these plans as an important part of the learning, and allows a sense of ownership and pride for the child.

Containment within a book does away with the need for lots of bits of paper that can be lost, look disorganised or not actually reflect the thinking, reasoning, predictions, plans, depth and richness of the learning.

A scrapbook is not a book where only the best work is completed; it is a true working document where children can practise, design and write about their experiences as a tool and as part of hands-on learning. Children take responsibility for these books and recognise them as an authentic part of their learning, play and project work.

Journals and portfolios

These are the child's record of some of the investigations, ideas, work and learning that occurs. They may contain photographs, written examples and some of the design briefs.

A journal or portfolio differs from a scrapbook in that the child and teacher gather together examples of work that can become part of assessment, reporting and sharing with parents. While scrapbooks can also be used in this way, the scrapbook is based on processes and works in progress rather than finished tasks or investigations.

Noticeboards

Children are encouraged to leave notes or notices for each other, for parents or teachers. Usually a small notepad is stuck to the noticeboard for children to take pieces of paper from and write notes.

Children take great delight in writing messages for their teacher or parents, and it promotes an enormous amount of writing and oral language experience.

Listening post

Not only can children listen to stories but they can also record their own voices, languages and conversations. They love listening back to their voices and this can be linked to storytelling, narrative and oral language practice. Having small books of empty pages in the area can facilitate children to write their language or draw or represent the stories they hear.

Letterboxes

Letterboxes are similar to noticeboards. Children can write to each other or leave notes for the teacher and these become a regular part of the classroom.

The letterboxes each display the child's name and can be used in a variety of ways by teachers and children. Children have the opportunity to post notes or letters to each other and the teacher can use them for additional activities. Notes can be written from the teacher and children can write notes to their parents.

As an alternative, provide pegs for children to attach notes to.

Small group and whole group experiences

In addition to individual or small groups working on investigations, there may be specific activities that lend themselves to some additional concepts to which teachers wish to expose all children.

A whole class may be engaged in this type of activity together rather than their separate investigations. However, this is for the minority rather than the majority of time and there will still be scope for children to demonstrate their skills and understandings in open ended ways rather than all completing the same worksheet.

Cooking

Cooking provides the opportunity for reading and researching cookbooks, making recipes, listing ingredients, following the instructions and of course actually cooking! Cooking is a great activity to conduct regularly with small groups in the classroom and is the type of activity that a parent helper can supervise and work with alongside with the children.

Surveying and data collection

Children can collect information with their clipboards on all sorts of things that interest them or are introduced by the teacher, for example, collecting information on favourite foods, the sorts of projects children are interested in, or ideas from others. This can link into literacy and numeracy as a truly integrated learning experience.

Producing a play or a film

Children often spontaneously take on the role of teacher, parent or other adult in the community. Often we can scaffold these opportunities and extend them into writing or recording the words of the play. Sometimes the play is enough in its own right and is providing rich oral language development. However, extending this into writing a script, and filming or photographing the play, is something that children love to do at times. They love to look at themselves.

Collating photos and samples of work for presentation

These presentations (which children can help to collate during the week) are snapshots of some of the investigations that children have been working on during each week. Some of these are selected to review and reflect on as a whole group toward the end of a week and can be used in the following ways:

- on an electronic whiteboard, children and teacher can review and write descriptions of the learning
- on A3-sized sheets, children and teacher can progress through the different photos

- teachers can make individual books from the reflections.

Personal reading books

These may include pictures or design briefs the children wish to present as a narrative or instruction manual for others to read about their work. They could be photos of the child's constructions and investigations that are turned into a book for reading or taken home to share with parents.

Big books

The children's work and photos of their projects can be made into a big book for reading with the teacher. Children engage more quickly in books and texts that they instantly relate to and recognise.

Easels

These can be used for design briefs, plans and maps that link to construction, blocks, pastings and ideas. Provide paint or Textas, pens, pencils, and a range of different writing mediums.

Whiteboard

Children develop a sense and expectation that writing is part of and linked to speaking. Recording events, plans and instructions can happen in a variety of ways, including through the modelling of the teacher. Whiteboards can be used to list:

- discussion topics for the morning session
- some of the tasks or projects that children are working on
- a sequence of expectations for the morning
- names for a clinic group
- some prompts or reminders.

Writer's workshop table

Provide access to a range of writing and reading materials. Children can use a workshop table as a resource area to link with purposeful and meaningful experiences they may wish to record or write about.

Books and posters for research, reading and enjoyment

Utilising a wide range of books is an important part of a WLA. Many teachers access public libraries to ensure a rich and broad range of books, texts and posters are available, and these become an integral part of the learning environment both inside and outside the classroom.

Placing books alongside children's investigations about dinosaurs and having posters depicting and representing some of the investigations of the children helps them to make links between the actual investigation and print, reading, writing and numeracy.

Signs

These are part of WLA learning and are used in a variety of forms to link literacy and numeracy with investigations. Signs that may describe the work being constructed, names of the children engaged in the particular investigation or provide instructions on how to use a particular investigation, are all part of enriching the learning environment.

Specific numeracy materials

Setting up the learning environment to promote rich experiences in numeracy requires a range of materials and resources that are accessible to children at all times. These include:

- tape measures
- rulers
- cups and jugs for measuring
- water troughs
- scales
- cash registers
- scanners
- obstacle courses
- outdoor and indoor blocks
- Lego
- Kapla
- boxes
- materials for filling and emptying
- material to take apart
- prop boxes (including supermarket materials, carpenter materials, plumber materials, etc.)

The teacher's role

The role of the adult is to plan carefully to promote opportunities for rich engagement in literacy and numeracy and to scaffold, instruct and extend when appropriate. While still using formal instruction for literacy and numeracy skills, the WLA does not advocate the use of:

- worksheets that have colouring in and stencilled letters and numbers
- cloned and structured writing.

Promoting rich oral language and conversation with children

Sharing with others about learning and interests

This does not have to occur in a lengthy show and tell session, which can lead to many children becoming disengaged. It can be spontaneous during their investigations, during reflection time (as a freebie), and in small groups with each other and the teacher.

Describing objects, events and relations

This occurs in many ways during the investigations of the children. Discussions with each other, problem solving, their attempts to sort through or understand particular things, developing research skills and attempting to construct particular things all provide children with many opportunities to describe and discuss.

Expressing feelings in words

Self-expression through appropriate verbal articulation is enhanced through children's investigations. They are often asked to reflect on not just the learning or investigation, but on how they feel, their emotions, frustrations and excitement about their projects.

Having one's own language modelled and spoken

Children who have English as second language require more oral language experience. They also require opportunities to have tapes and stories in their first language to enhance and consolidate their first language as well as many opportunities to model and practise English through interactions with others.

Having fun with language

Children require time to experiment with language, to create nonsense rhymes and stories, to play with language and writing and to construct and create language that is fun.

Using measuring tapes in play

Children can use tapes, balls of string or rulers to measure their block buildings and draw and measure distances in many aspects of their constructions and investigations.

Scales, weighing, time

In dramatic play areas such as a hospital, restaurant or home corner, children can weigh ingredients or dolls, write appointment times for the doctors, use clocks to work out times for visit or make money for the shop.

Summary

- Literacy and numeracy are integrated into children's investigations.

- Formal literacy and numeracy instruction is still used, but attempts in most cases to model or instruct using meaningful examples from the interests and investigations of the children.

- Examples from investigations and the children's interests are used by the teacher as a springboard into formal teaching sessions.

- Small clinic groups, guided reading and instruction sessions are still integrated into the day or week.

- Writing, reading, researching and recording experiences are all integrated into the children's investigations.

- Literacy and numeracy are embedded around the learning environment and many resources are provided for linking children's investigations with writing, researching and reading.

- Clipboards, scrapbooks, journals and portfolios are all utilised for the children's design briefs, plans and attempts.

- Photographs are a major part of modelling, writing stories and reading together about the children's investigations.

- A range of numeracy resources are accessible at all times, providing spontaneous moments of scaffolding during children's investigations.

Chapter 10
Personalised and inclusive learning

'As we grow in awareness of one another ... a wonderful thing begins to happen: we begin to care for the other as if the other is part of us. This is the magic of life that our ancient teachers have bid us to see; the invisible filaments of interconnectedness that bind us together in love and appreciation.'

Scott A. Hunt

Introduction

In all communities and classrooms there is a range of children who reflect diversity. This diversity includes aspects such as learning styles, personalities, cultures, language, abilities, disabilities, health and behaviours.

The essence of the WLA is that we respect and acknowledge that not all children are the same. The WLA has been designed to reflect in everyday practice that not all children are ready or able to learn the same thing in the same way at the same time. The WLA takes a non-deficit approach in relation to diversity of all kinds. In other words, rather than assume that there is one norm that all children generally fit within and that any children outside that norm are automatically assumed to be not normal (and therefore all grouped together as challenging), the WLA's starting point is that diversity is the norm. Some children along the continuum will require slightly different supports or strategies at times to greater or lesser degrees. In order to ensure equity of learning opportunities, it is important to recognise differences along that continuum so that each child's own set of strengths, needs and learning requirements are met appropriately.

Children with special or additional needs

The WLA is based on a general set of principles as described in Chapter 3 that reflect developmentally appropriate practices. These principles and practices are specifically and proactively inclusive of the range of abilities and additional needs that children reflect in learning environments.

In the past few years, the WLA has been implemented not only into mainstream classes which have children with a range of special and additional needs but also in special education schools. Questions or queries often arise from staff who may either teach within a special education setting or have children in their mainstream classroom with additional needs as they embark on introducing the WLA. These include:

- 'What about the children who need structure and routine such as children with Asperger's syndrome or on the autism spectrum?'
- 'Won't the investigation time be too noisy for them?'
- 'How will these children be able to make a choice and settle when they find it difficult to make decisions?'
- 'I have children who are not intellectually able to adequately think through how to make a decision. What happens to them?'
- ''I have a child who has extreme behavioural aggression. How will this child be able to cope with the freedom around the room at investigation time?'
- 'I have a child who just cannot sit still at any group times. How will this work in relation to tuning in and reflection time and being a focus child?'
- 'I have a child with Asperger's syndrome and he just returns to the same learning experience each morning. What do I do to move him forward or extend him?'
- 'I have some children who cannot easily move around the room due to their physical needs. What happens to them?'

Before addressing these questions and providing some strategies that will support teachers who may have children with specific additional needs or requirements, it is worth sharing the experiences of teachers, parents and leaders in schools who have witnessed what actually does happen for children with additional needs within the WLA approach.

'Investigations is the only part of the day where this child who has Asperger's is actually most settled, with the least behavioural issues arising.'

'The morning session of investigations provides the most lovely and relaxed start to the day for this little boy. He usually has

great difficulty in settling, being focused and behaving. Investigations give him the time and space to move into the day more gently.'

'All the children see this particular child in a position of success each day. Instead of highlighting all the things he can't do, the children see all the things he does do so well and happily during investigations. It is the one part of the day where everyone succeeds and no one stands out as being different in a negative way.'

'I find I have more time rather than less to help the children with additional needs. My relationship with them is significantly enhanced as investigation times provide more time for me to work with them individually as well as to encourage them to work and investigate alongside others.'

'I have found that the other children in the class seem to view and experience this little girl not through her disability but through all the things she makes and creates during investigation time. They see her as one of them—the same, not different.'

'It is the time of day when it is least obvious or noticeable that any of the children may have a special need.'

The nature of investigations as described throughout the book provides experiences and opportunities for children to work at their own level, and to reflect their own interests, capabilities, creativeness and timing. It is an unrushed and unhurried part of the day where time can be pitched to meet the needs of all children.

The open-ended nature of the experiences means that while children are challenged to extend, think, problem-solve, take some risks, be creative and work not just independently but alongside others, they are also not set up to fail in these experiences, rather to succeed at whatever their level and capability is.

Ensuring all children can work effectively during investigation sessions

There are some key factors of the WLA, particularly the investigation sessions, which assist all children—including those with particular additional needs—to work effectively and constructively and to feel a sense of routine and predictability.

Routine structure and predictability

When first hearing about the WLA, many people assume it is simply like a free Friday afternoon or wet weather type of play session where children choose everything they want to do without any structure or guidance from staff. As explained in Chapter 3, the WLA is a very rigorous pedagogy that has 'non-negotiable' core elements in order to ensure the approach works effectively and with integrity for all children and staff.

All children in their early years require routines, structure and predictability each day, but this can be particularly important for children with additional psychological, practical or behavioural needs. The more predictable and routine the day, the easier it is for young children and children with special needs to adjust, adapt and work within the classroom environment.

Checklist for ensuring routine, structure and predictability at investigation time

- Investigation occurs at the beginning of each morning for at least four mornings each week.

- Tuning in follows the same format each morning including:

    - welcome and housekeeping/general discussion

- quick revision and reflection about the current learning in all areas including literacy and numeracy

- revisiting the current learning intentions

- focus children, reporter and photographer are scaffolded

- dispersal time models some intention and ideas from students before they leave to commence their investigations.

- At dispersal time, children who require additional help with planning or making a decision about where they will start will meet for an extra few minutes with the staff who will scaffold and guide them to develop their intention. At times the teacher may have to help the child make a decision, show them options, walk with them or help them get started.

- During investigation time, focus children, reporter and photographer each spend some time with the teacher.

- After time with focus children, the teacher then assists with any other children and may at this time ensure the children with additional needs are on track.

- Reflection time must always follow the same format: focus children, reporter and photographer, followed by any incidental 'freebies'.

- Packing away and organising is always held after reflection time is completed.

Additional strategies to assist with children who have special needs

Individual schedules

Some children require an individual schedule that helps them to work their way through the day or session. Some children may also require their own schedule to help them with investigations. Many schools use a version of these schedules with all children.

Mini contracts

Some children respond well to a 'mini contract'. These contracts are not used in a negative way. In fact, they can become very popular with all children in the group. A mini contract is held on a clipboard and invites the child to decide (in consultation with or at the direction of the teacher) which area of investigations they may start with first. This provides a lovely time for the teacher to have a conversation and relationship-building time with the child and helps the child feel a little important that they are given their own special contract. Contracts may simply state, 'Kathy is going to start in the block area today' and are signed off by the teacher and the child. These contracts often help children who find it very difficult to self-select, to organise themselves or who simply feel overwhelmed with choices.

Note: these contracts are not used frequently, and are not usually given to children simply because they take time to make decisions. In fact, being able to make decisions, follow through and persist are skills that children need time and opportunity to practise.

Buddies

Sometimes, the teacher may buddy a child with another child so that they can still 'report' or be the photographer with some help. This also helps the buddy to enjoy working alongside another child and to have practice in assisting children who may have different levels of skills or abilities.

Learning environment

Ensuring that the environment, defined spaces, and the classroom in general are well-organised, tidy and uncluttered is very important. This helps all children be familiar and comfortable with their learning environment and to be able to work within it safely and comfortably. A messy, disorganised, understimulating or overstimulating physical environment will lead to messy, disengaged and disruptive behaviours in children. The more organised the room, the easier it is for all children to work constructively within it. Setting up the environment with cosy corners and defined spaces and using boards, shelving, material, netting, as discussed in Chapter 5 all help to define spaces for children and provide some personal space which often helps them feel secure.

Some children may need and respond at various times to their own special space and place to work. Organising a particular small table or area where they can work, or where they can bring things to and from often helps them to focus, to not feel overwhelmed or become overexcited.

The WLA caters very easily and proactively for children with a variety of diverse needs. It specifically personalises the learning opportunities during investigation time through the range of open-ended materials and experiences that are made available every day for all children. This is the essence of the strength and success of the approach. It personalises learning and meets individual abilities and disabilities without making them obvious or special or in a deficit manner.

Children from diverse backgrounds, including Indigenous communities within Australia

The WLA is now a major teaching and learning approach across Australia. It is used in Indigenous communities in Arnhem Land, in inner-city refugee communities with limited English, and in all forms of rural, remote and metropolitan communities where there is a huge mix of children and families from a range of cultures and countries.

In some of the communities with which I have worked—particularly the remote parts of Australia—Indigenous elders have given feedback on how they perceive the WLA and in particular the investigation times. Many of the elders have commented on how pleasing it has been to witness the start of each day providing experiences of active interactions and explorations that engage children rather than disengage them. They say that 'The children want to come to school now' and 'They have fun now and learn more easily'. Similarly, teachers often remark on how children are more eager to attend and participate in school now that the day starts with investigations.

The WLA emphasis is on respecting, including and incorporating children's own cultural experiences, language and family backgrounds. Research from around the world stresses that in order for children to competently and successfully acquire English, they must be able to be immersed in their own family language and to have elements of their language and culture within the learning environment (Clarke 1992). Studies also indicate that if a child is immersed in their own family language, they are much more likely to develop correct grammar and vocabulary in English.

The mistake that many policy makers and governments often make is to assume that in order to ensure effective literacy, numeracy and language, children's own home languages must not be used within the learning environment. This is incorrect and defies studies that indicate that children must have access to using their own language as well as to be introduced to and have English modelled in their learning environment (Clarke 1999).

Children's family language is part of their culture and sense of identity and belonging. The WLA has a specifically designed range of strategies that work within and alongside the investigations, which promote respect and inclusion of culturally appropriate experiences and materials, alongside opportunities for rich English speaking, listening and reading practice every session.

The WLA also acknowledges that many families have different prior experiences or expectations about school and learning in the home and outside of the school environment. For some groups, the notion of sitting still in a classroom with things to write on each day is not part of how their own homes and communities work. Some children may have more structure in their homes than in a traditional classroom. Some communities have a much stronger emphasis on physical activity, active engagement and exploration. Some communities have a rich oral history and emphasise verbal language over print. Some cultural groups place a greater emphasis on didactic rote learning and some cultural groups have the opposite emphasis.

The WLA has been designed to respect individuals and personalise learning as much as possible. It recognises that for all children, but particularly for children from different cultural and linguistic backgrounds, the opportunities for them to speak, listen, engage and participate in real life, hands-on investigations is extremely important.

Common questions when working with children from diverse backgrounds, including Indigenous communities

How can the children participate in the role of focus child or reporter if they cannot speak English?

Often the children are given a camera and simply asked to take some photos. Sometimes they are partnered with another child to work together. At reflection time, the children can show photos or examples of what they have been making. Other children are encouraged to make comments. English is most often spoken at this time with the child even if they cannot understand much of what is being said.

How will they have opportunities to practise English if they are speaking their own language to each other during investigations?

Children will have exposure to English during tuning in, reflection, time spent with the teacher and with other children. They will strengthen their own language speaking to others in their home language and this is a productive part of early language development rather than a problem. English is strengthened if children have good grammar and vocabulary in their home language first.

How will they acquire English if we let them speak their own language?

Children are more likely to acquire correct grammar, comprehension and vocabulary in English if they have a strong and correct expression of their own home language first.

Is there a need to reflect Indigenous and other cultural/ethnic influences in the learning environment if we don't have children from these backgrounds?

Yes. Part of ensuring children develop as good global citizens involves exposing them to the wide range of cultural backgrounds and Indigenous languages that make up the diversity of the world.

This is important no matter where the school is located. Ideally, learning environments always reflect a rich range of diversity in relation to culture, languages and experiences.

These experiences should be an inclusive and integrated range of books, texts, posters, songs and stories that are not used as tokenistic add-ons to the curriculum; they should be part of the range of experiences that are provided to all children. In other words, teachers should always avoid 'doing Aborigines' or 'doing Indonesia'. This perpetuates a stereotyped view that these cultures and countries are somehow studied separately instead of just being part of the cultural diversity we find in everyday life.

How do we include culturally relevant materials and experiences into ordinary classroom activities?

I recently observed a Grade 1 boy from an Indigenous community in Arnhem Land dancing with a rubbish bin lid. He was using the lid as a drum and he had painted his face with ordinary paint. One of the elders informed me that he was dancing a version of a corroboree that he had observed the community perform in recent days. All learning environments require a range of music, instruments, artefacts and experiences that can lend themselves to the diversity of culture so that children can utilise these materials to express their own cultural experiences. In addition, texts, posters, songs and activities need to reflect experiences from around the world, which helps avoids stereotypical activities.

Similarities within differences

Regardless of experience and culture, all children in their early childhood years reflect some similar elements of early childhood:

- all children have a natural inclination to learn through exploration, investigation and play

- all children's brain development requires opportunities to engage with concrete, real materials where they can manipulate objects, create, act out roles they have observed and construct and make meaning through their play and active engagement

- all children require time that is not rushed or hurried

- all children require time to adapt and readjust to the next session or lesson

- all children require one-on-one time with adults to establish and firm up relationships and trust within the learning environment

- all children require opportunities for ordinary conversations to enhance the relationship between language and thinking skills.

Providing appropriate cultural and linguistic experiences for all children

- Ensure that musical experiences of all kinds deliberately portray and represent the diversity of culture and language, regardless of whether or not children from different cultures are part of the learning environment.

- Ensure that when children from other cultures are within the learning environment that aspects of their own culture and language are included as part of the experiences provided.

- Include and invite parents to come and share or participate in the learning environment. They may have particular foods, music, stories or games from their own culture that they can introduce and share with the children.

- Be careful not to portray all Indigenous communities as the same. Avoid representations suggesting that all Australian Indigenous paintings are dots, that all music includes a didgeridoo or that all Indigenous people live in remote areas of the country. If you have Indigenous children and families within the community ensure you understand what languages they may speak and be respectful of the unique aspects of their culture.

- Always have a range of culturally appropriate artefacts, utensils and objects that can be used as part of dramatic play of all kinds. Avoid simply thinking of setting up a home corner with chopsticks and bowls. This is far too simplistic. You might include chopsticks with forks and spoons so that children have a range of different tools within one experience in a more integrated and holistic way.

Summary

- Personalised learning and responding to and respecting the vast range of diversity in children, families and the community is an integral aspect of a rich, rewarding and appropriate education for all children.

- Regardless of need, strength, culture, ability, disability or experience, the WLA provides a systematic model of ensuring that all children are able to fully participate in learning without feeling a sense of failure or irrelevance to their own lives.

Chapter 11
Informing and educating parents

'The central task of education is to implant a will and facility for learning; it should produce not learned but learning people. The truly human society is a learning society, where grandparents, parents and children are students together.'

Eric Hoffer

Introduction

With any change in a school community or classroom, parents require information, time and opportunities to discuss, question and observe what the changes look like and how they impact on their child's learning. In addition, staff also require support, information and strategies to help them introduce the approach.

> *Leadership is an important aspect of the change process. Leadership must provide information and support to teachers, and work productively and proactively with the parent community alongside the teachers. To do this, leadership needs to participate in the professional development of the staff and the leadership needs to understand the philosophy, the key principles and the core elements of the WLA.*

Introducing the WLA into the early years of school (particularly as it looks similar to an informal preschool experience) can sometimes cause parental anxiety. They may view the investigations as less academically rigorous than what they expect in a traditional classroom.

Interestingly, it often seems that unless a parent is a teacher or has studied education themselves, they tend to think of 'real' or 'effective' learning as being similar to their own school experience. Despite perhaps not having even enjoyed their school experiences, some parents may hold a view that effective learning is highly structured, with children sitting quietly and all doing the same thing at the same time.

Even many preschool teachers have trouble convincing parents that learning through active, hands-on investigations results in greater levels of engagement, motivation and actual skill acquisition.

Particularly in our current society, with an emphasis on benchmarks, standards and outcomes, parents can feel that the WLA may not be rigorous enough or that their children may not get the results that are needed.

It is very important that schools or teams of teachers implementing the WLA are clear about what the philosophy is, how it enhances learning and how results and standards are still met. In fact our data indicates that not only is learning, engagement and motivation increased through the WLA, but also that oral language, literacy and numeracy are all enhanced and most significantly sustained beyond the early years.

The WLA approach is extremely rigorous and filled with teacher direction, scaffolding, extension and intervention. Parents therefore need to feel able to understand the approach, what research indicates and how it links directly to literacy, numeracy, social skills and all areas of learning.

Suggested strategies and processes for parent information

1. Once a decision has been made to introduce the WLA and staff are feeling ready and confident it is helpful to inform parents that some of the teaching and learning strategies may appear more open-ended, hands-on and creative. Reassure them that skill instruction is still being used.

2. Provide parents with an appropriate reading about the WLA (see the parent helper information sheet on the CD) and let them know that many schools across the country use the approach so they feel reassured that it is not an experiment that is setting a precedent or that it is only your school and a few others that are implementing the approach.

3. Hold a parent information session after one term, when staff are feeling confident in their implementation journey. It is highly recommended that the school uses a WLA accredited mentor who is familiar with the approach and has experience talking to parent groups. A parent information session can help on a number of levels:

- it helps the community to see you are linked with professionals and experts who know and can clearly articulate the message

- it helps support the staff and speak on their behalf, reinforcing teaching expertise

- it provides a model for the teachers to assist them in further discussions

- it invites questions issues or concerns to be directed to someone who is not actually teaching their child. Often parents feel better able to challenge or question an outsider and it is important they are not only given this opportunity but that staff are also supported.

4. Halfway through the year, provide a brief parent survey as an opportunity for parents to articulate their responses to their children's learning. Use open-ended questions such as:

    - What aspects of your child's schooling do you think they most enjoy?

    - How do you perceive your child's learning and attitude toward school?

    - What do you think are the greatest strengths of the current program at school?

5. Place the fortnightly SOI printed on A3 paper in a visible and easily accessible position. Print the developmental domains and learning intentions from the SOI in large font on the noticeboard or door of the classroom so parents can see explicit learning and teaching is planned for on a regular basis. These can be copied and pasted directly from the SOI.

6. Send home books, photos and examples of the learning and skills that have been acquired by the children. Try to describe the learning, rather than the actual investigation itself. Focus children each week can be a way of sending something home regularly.

Developmental and learning objectives for fortnight commencing 16 March, Term 1: Prep grade examples for parents

Social:

- for the children to begin to work alongside others and get to know each other.

Emotional:

- for the children to feel confident and emotionally safe in their new environment.

Physical:

- for the children to learn to move around the space, indoors and outdoors safely and well coordinated.

Language:

- for the children to begin to feel able to verbalise their needs or wants to the teacher and each other.

Cognitive:

- for the children to engage in creative investigations.

Literacy:

- for the children to recognise their own names and for some children to write them.

Numeracy:

- for the children to classify and group objects.

Other:

- for the children to be introduced to the range of specialist classes and routines of the school and classroom.

> A photo might be sent home with the child working in the vet clinic that the children made. The teacher might write, 'During the vet clinic dramatic play, a number of skills were being demonstrated and practised which were later used for more formal skill instruction:
>
> - oral language
> - extension of vocabulary
> - writing lists and handwriting practice
> - negotiating skills with others
> - counting money for payment
> - reading information about pets and animals
> - designing a care plan for the pet.'

7. Always be proactive. Don't assume that because one cohort of parents seemed to understand and support the WLA that the information sessions don't need to occur each year. Reinforcing and revisiting the WLA is a constant need.

8. When parent helpers are present, show them some of your plan, the adult role and some of the key learning intentions. This helps the parent to make the link between investigations and the learning and also provides them with some ideas of how their conversations and interactions can scaffold the learning. See the CD appendix for a parent helper information sheet.

9. Using the term 'WLA' rather than 'play' helps parents to see that play is a tool used for learning, based on an actual curriculum model.

10. Remember that leadership must support and reinforce the approach. If a parent is having particular difficulty in understanding or accepting the approach, always refer them to the principal who can support you.

11. Provide a parent library that has a few texts about the curriculum as well as some copies of research and websites the parent or carer can look up themselves for further information.

Overview of key WLA principles

Listed below are a number of the key elements of the WLA and implications for practice.

- *Children's interests are used as the predominant means for learning experiences.*

- *Children's interests are expanded, scaffolded and supported as a means of ongoing engagement in particular learning areas.*

- *Additional events or concepts at a community or school level are incorporated within the planning document but not viewed or used as the 'topic' or 'theme' on which planning is based or all experiences are planned.*

- *Investigative experiences are the major pedagogical tool for teaching and learning, alongside formal instruction.*

- *The nature of experiences promotes creativity, imagination and scope for the child to invent and create, and avoid cloned art work, worksheets and stencils.*

- *Planning documentation identifies objectives for the children's development in the first instance and in addition, identifies key learning intentions and children's interests as a basis for planning learning experiences.*

- *The learning experiences emphasise active engagement, provide children with opportunities to explore processes not just end products and seek to encourage children to pursue some of their learning experiences into ongoing projects for either short or longer periods of time.*

- *Teachers observe and document key skills, needs, strengths and interests of individual children and use these to plan and implement appropriate experiences*

- *and set further learning and developmental intentions.*

- *While skill instruction sessions and small and large group times are still used within the classroom, literacy, numeracy and other areas of learning are integrated within a range of learning experiences.*

- *Teachers must still direct, scaffold, extend or intervene with children in order to ensure that they are actively engaged and learning.*

- *The notion of 'integrated curriculum' within the WLA refers to all learning areas being recognised as integrated and embedded in children's learning and not a discrete part of the day where a particular content or focus area is used.*

- *A balance is set by the teacher from what emerges from the children in response to the range of experiences provided and what the teacher wishes to introduce to the children in relation to skill and content.*

- *In practice, the WLA uses a mix throughout the day of active hands-on investigations, group times, personal reflection times, skill instruction and other learning experiences provided by the school.*

Parents can be a great source of support in the WLA. Parents often collect junk materials or provide old sofas or cushions for home corners and other dramatic play resources. Sometimes the talents and expertise of parents can be utilised if some of the children express an interest in a particular investigation.

Helping parents to understand and accept the WLA will build stronger and more positive links between home and school. (Common concerns and misunderstandings of parents are listed with responses in Chapter 12.) One of the most effective strategies for helping parents to feel comfortable with the approach is to ensure a consistent message through the team. In some cases, if one teacher is using the approach and another teacher is using a more structured, traditional approach, a point of comparison can be made by parents and this leads to significant problems across the school. It is highly recommended that a whole team adopts the WLA.

That is why a whole-school approach or at least a whole team approach is recommended. It helps all teachers share, learn and experience the approach together. In addition, it also sets a consistent model and philosophy across the school or year level.

Summary

- Leadership knowledge of the WLA and support is essential for supporting teachers and informing parents about the WLA.

- Parents need to be informed through a variety of strategies including written information, information sessions held by external WLA accredited mentors and displays of learning intentions each fortnight.

- Parent helpers require an information sheet and session to help them understand the approach and how to work with the children during their investigations.

- Whole teams need to implement the WLA to reduce comparison and competition in parents' minds between conflicting approaches occurring in the same school.

- Conducting parent surveys twice a year helps parents feel they are given the opportunity to comment and helps teachers and leadership gauge how the parents are viewing the approach.

Chapter 12
Frequently asked questions

What happens to formal literacy and numeracy blocks?

Discrete times for formal instruction are still required, but times are flexible and do not necessarily have to occur in one solid block each day. Many schools use different aspects of literacy and numeracy at different times throughout the day. This helps children to concentrate in smaller blocks of time, and provides a freer and more responsive approach to formal teaching times based upon the dynamic of the day, the mood of the children and other aspects of the day or week.

What about literacy rotations?

Rotations do not always provide children with time to engage, explore and enjoy their learning or to complete it. Lots of short rotations in each literacy session (or in any other aspect of the WLA) are not required or desirable.

Will the children be ready for moving into the next grade at the end of the year and will they reach the standards or benchmarks expected of them?

The WLA does not get children ready earlier or later than other approaches. Either a child will be ready and at a particular standard or they won't. Our data indicates that the same percentage of children who would reach particular standards in other approaches will reach them in the WLA. However, our own experience also indicates that children will enjoy their schooling more, engage more meaningfully, attend more regularly and increase a range of pro-social and oral language skills more significantly within the WLA.

What if children don't initiate any of their own ideas?

Children moving straight from a preschool year are used to initiating their own ideas. However, it is true that sometimes it is more difficult for some children to think of particular ideas. This is where the teacher can scaffold and suggest ideas that may trigger some interest in the child and guide the child to developing intent.

What if children go back to the same activity each time?

Children actually often return to the same or a similar activity. This is not necessarily a negative or unproductive thing. Through repetition, practice and experimentation children often acquire and refine skills and thinking as well as understandings.

Teachers can often add to the area of interest if they think the child needs extending or moving on, rather than expecting the child to leave their point of interest.

How do I know if what I am observing is readiness or willingness?

This is a question that always faces us as teachers. Knowing more about the child, their maturity and their experiences helps us to ascertain if and when the child is ready or in need of further scaffolding, or alternatively, needs further time before being moved on.

What are the developmental domains and how important are they?

These represent the 'whole' child. They consider the emotional, social, linguistic, cognitive and physical aspects of the child and are of equal importance to literacy, numeracy and other learning objectives. The domains help us to plan appropriate experiences based on the stage of maturity of the children.

Are formal instruction, whole groups and clinic groups still used?

Yes, formal instruction is still used every day. The role of the teacher is still one of scaffolding, extending, intervening, modelling, observing and interacting with the children. As much as possible, the formal instruction sessions use some of the interests or investigations of children to help engagement and motivation.

How can I fit investigations into an already crowded curriculum and busy schedule?

The investigations are an integral and major part of every day, where children continue to build on their interests and learning. This time is not squeezed into an existing day and timetable. The timetable changes completely to accommodate this approach which is a total philosophy and pedagogy in its own right. The WLA is a pedagogy that always uses a mix of formal teaching and individual investigation time. You can't have one without the other.

What if some staff in the team don't want to do it?

Staff need to be given time, support, professional development and understanding so that through the implementation phase all staff have the opportunity to find out more information and to accept the approach. The importance of leadership, decision making and philosophical commitment to the approach is paramount. It is impossible to have one team member opposing or doing something different from the rest of the team. A consistent model and philosophy must be endorsed by the leadership and used by all those in the teaching team.

How will the parents feel assured that their children are still learning and we are still teaching?

There are a number of ways to help parents to feel comfortable and understand the approach. Parent education information sessions, displaying the developmental domain intentions and learning intentions each fortnight and inviting parents in to see how the approach works are some strategies that help. Chapter 11 provides more detail on this.

What happens to boys in this approach?

This approach is a real winner for boys. Their particular stages of maturity and development are often not consistent with traditional expectations of all sitting together and being still for long periods of time. Boys are actively engaged and motivated in this approach and set up to succeed and enjoy the learning environment.

What happens to girls in this approach?

The approach provides a wide range of opportunities and experiences for both boys and girls. Girls are equally engaged in experiences that they relate to and find interesting and relevant.

How does it fit with other approaches like Reggio Emilia or enquiry learning?

This is a total approach, philosophy and pedagogy in its own right. It is an approach developed in Australia, but may be implemented successfully in any number of cultural and educational contexts across the world. While elements of other pedagogical tools can be used (including elements of Steiner or Montessori), the core elements of the pedagogy are child development and active engagement through children's interests alongside formal instruction.

Common concerns or misunderstandings of parents

It won't suit my child. They need direction

Children are still directed but also encouraged to practice the skills of self-direction which is an important element of being a successful learner.

There is no structure in the room

There is an enormous amount of structure, routine, expectation and responsibility within the environment.

The children can do anything they like and may never choose to do anything to extend themselves

Teachers still direct, scaffold and extend children. Children are never left without direction and purpose. Sometimes the child decides and sometimes the teacher decides.

How can literacy and numeracy be learned through play?

Literacy and numeracy are an integral aspect of everyday life. Formal skill instruction is still used within the pedagogy, but many rich and broad opportunities for literacy and numeracy are embedded into the investigations and utilised by the teacher through relevant and meaningful experiences.

We can't always choose to do whatever we like in life. Isn't there too much choice and not enough practice in following directions and doing what you are told to do?

Making choices and following through responsibly with decisions is also an important part of life. Problem solving, taking risks and bouncing back when things don't quite work out are all part of successful lifelong learning. The WLA still has limits and expectations and is not always about the child's choice. Sometimes it is led by the teacher.

How do teachers know what standard each child is at if they are all doing different things?

The way teachers plan, as well as the core elements of the approach (like the focus children, clinics groups and the range of assessment and observation tools) used is part of a whole model that ensures teachers are monitoring and supporting each child. In fact, this model results in very high levels of teacher knowledge of individual children and their learning.

I can't see the value in constructing, pasting and dramatic play. Where is the learning?

There are various skills that children practise and learn through these experiences. Conversation, language, thinking, creativity, fine motor, maths concepts, reading, writing and investigating are all skills that are essential to being a successful learner. Refer to Chapter 2 for more information.

What happens when they move out of the early years classrooms and into Grade 3?

Children are able to adapt quickly to changes in their environment. Many schools actually continue the WLA into Grades 3–6, albeit with a different slant. Even for those who do not, the children move into the new environment and take on the different classroom rules, just like they adapt to different teaching styles and personalities.

How will they reach the benchmark if they can just play all day?

There is no system in the world that can make a child reach a benchmark in a meaningful and sustainable way before they are ready. The number of children who reach benchmarks in the old system will be the same as those who reach them in this system. Intervention, extension and extra supports are still provided for children who require these.

This could only work effectively with lots of parent helpers or two teachers as in preschool

The nature of the investigations lend themselves to children being able to attend, self-regulate and involve themselves without the practical help of an adult to make the investigation successful. No activity is set up that must require an adult, such as cooking, knitting or sewing, unless an additional adult is in the room.

Appendices

Developmental domains

the Walker Learning Approach
DEVELOPMENTALLY APPROPRIATE PRACTICE

Emotional domain	Social domain	Cognitive domain	Language domain	Physical domain
• refers to a range of elements of maturity centred around the individual • relates intentions within general stages of development expectations	• refers to a range of elements of maturity centred around the individual in relation to others • relates objectives within general stage of development expectations	• refers to a range of elements related to thinking and making sense of the world	• refers to elements of expression and articulation in communication	• refers to elements related to gross motor, fine motor and bilateral coordination including spatial awareness • also includes body image, health and nutrition
• self-expression • expression of needs and/or wants • ability to describe or explain feelings or frustrations • assertion • speaking on behalf of oneself • recognising needs • verbalising opinions • ability to question • ability to reflect on self, strengths and challenges • self-concept • self-esteem • self-competence • resilience • attachment, relationship maintenance and sustenance • sense of identity • trust • autonomy • independence and interdependence • sense of initiative and industry • decision making	• awareness of others • acceptance of diversity • interest in others • relationship development • initiating peer interaction • parallel, associative, collaborative and cooperative interactions • expressing thoughts and opinions with others • working alongside others • expressing needs to others • sharing views and opinions with others • recognising importance of interactions with others • developing empathy for others • developing respect for others • ability to share space, resources and people with others as appropriate	• creative thinking • perspective taking • lateral thinking • reflective thinking • problem solving • risk taking • planning • predicting • investigating • processing information • deductive thinking • reasoning • cause and effect • questioning • relationships between factors • concepts of time • positional language	• clarity of articulation • grammar • vocabulary • speech • volume of voice • intonation • expression through language • oral language experiences	• movement around indoor and outdoor environments • hand–eye coordination • handedness clarification and consolidation • muscle strength in hands, fingers and wrists • left–right coordination in walking, skipping, marching, climbing, etc. • pincer, palmer and mature tripod grips • upper body coordination

Play Matters 2nd Edition © Kathy Walker 2011

Key WLA principles

Listed below are a number of the key elements of the WLA and implications for practice.

- Children's interests are used as the predominant means for learning experiences during investigations. Teachers may add other ideas and concepts.
- Children's interests are expanded, scaffolded and supported as a means of ongoing engagement in particular learning areas.
- Additional issues or concepts at a community or school level are incorporated within the planning document but not viewed or used as the 'topic' or 'theme' on which planning is based or all experiences are planned.
- Investigative play-based experiences are the major pedagogical tool for teaching and learning alongside formal instruction.
- The nature of experiences promotes creativity, imagination and scope for children to invent and create and avoid cloned art work, worksheets and stencils.
- Planning documentation identifies intentions for the children's development in the first instance and in addition, identifies key learning intentions and children's interests as a basis for planning learning experiences.
- The learning experiences emphasise active engagement, provide children with opportunities to explore processes (not just end products) and seek to encourage children to pursue some of their learning experiences into ongoing projects for either short or longer periods of time.
- Observation and documentation by teachers of key skills, needs, strengths and interests of individual children is used to further plan and implement appropriate experiences and set further learning and developmental objectives.
- Formal skill instruction sessions and small and large group times are still used within the classroom in literacy, numeracy and other areas of learning. These skills are also integrated within a range of learning experiences.
- Teachers must still direct, scaffold, extend or intervene with children in order to ensure that children are actively engaged and learning.
- The notion of integrated curriculum within the WLA refers to all learning areas being recognised as integrated and embedded in children's learning and not as discrete parts of the day where a particular content or focus area is used.
- A balance is set by the teacher incorporating interests emerging from the child in response to experiences, and what the teacher wishes to introduce in relation to skill and content.
- In practice, the WLA uses a mix of active, hands-on investigative play-based work, alongside group times, personal reflection times, skill instruction and other learning experiences provided by the school each day.

Play Matters 2nd Edition © Kathy Walker 2011

Key procedures for implementing the WLA

Implementing the WLA in order to sustain the approach and to link successfully with all learning areas requires time and careful thought. These elements are strongly recommended:

Leadership

- understanding of the philosophy
- clarity of direction
- rationale for change
- timeline for implementation and strategies
- commitment to the philosophy
- support from leadership

Communication with staff

- discussion of values and beliefs about children, learning and teaching
- consideration of the implications for curriculum topics, reporting and assessment, timetabling
- whole-school overview to all staff (even those who are not in the year levels concerned)
- leadership meeting

Professional development

- child development theory
- implications of child development
- planning
- linking literacy and numeracy
- integrating the curriculum
- assessment
- reporting
- observation of developmental domains
- scaffolding at tuning in and reflection time
- setting up the learning environment

Discussion

- role of and planning implications for specialist teachers
- what happens to integrated curriculum?
- how and where does literacy and numeracy fit?
- types of play
- working effectively with parents
- setting up classrooms
- resources and budget considerations
- trialling the process
- mentoring and supports
- professional readings

Play Matters 2nd Edition © Kathy Walker 2011

Daily record sheet

Groups or individual names	Investigation	Ideas for extension/scaffolding	Additional resources

the Walker Learning Approach
DEVELOPMENTALLY APPROPRIATE PRACTICE

Play Matters 2nd Edition © Kathy Walker 2011

Statement of intent
Preschool to Grade 2

the Walker Learning Approach
DEVELOPMENTALLY APPROPRIATE PRACTICE

Developmental domain objectives	State/territory framework key outcomes	Learning objectives	Children's current interests	Staff/school/ community interests	Learning experiences	Modifications
Emotional		**Maths** Number			*Investigations*	
Social		Measurement				
Language		**Literacy** Speaking/listening			*Explicit teaching sessions*	
Cognitive		Writing				
Physical		Reading				

Play Matters 2nd Edition © Kathy Walker 2011

120 Play Matters

Individual record

Child's name:	Date of birth:

Development	
Social	
Emotional	
Cognitive	
Language	
Physical	
Developmental objective	

Key learning areas	
Literacy observation	
Literacy goal	
Numeracy observation	
Numeracy goal	

Key framework outcomes	
Specific interests/topics	
Additional information	
Parent comment	

Play Matters 2nd Edition © Kathy Walker 2011

Relief teacher WLA information sheet

Thank you for working in this classroom today. We use the Walker Learning Approach (WLA) which means some of the strategies listed below usually occur each day. The following is a general format for the day that you may like to follow.

Commencement of the day

Morning 'tuning in' with children (about 20 minutes)
There will be a focus child schedule on the noticeboard. Invite the focus children to share what they are currently or intending to be working on during their investigations. There will be a reporter and maybe a photographer—the teacher gives these children a task to report on and to photograph respectively. The tasks allocated to these children will be dependent on their stage of development and the learning intentions. At the end of the tuning in, the children to move off to the learning areas to start their investigations. The teacher disperses the children in small numbers and confirms with the children that they know where they are going and what they intend to investigate.

Investigation time (about 45 minutes)
Children can work in any of the learning areas by themselves or as small groups. They can choose where and what they are going to investigate. The teacher aims to scaffold the children from their interest so that they are supported and extended where appropriate. The teacher will spend the first half of investigations working with the focus children, reporter and photographer. Then the teacher will work with other children who need support, direction and or extension. Some children may need direction or suggestions for new ideas. Others will find their own work to do. The aim for the teacher is to sit and observe or support some of the children in their investigations.

Reflection with children (20 minutes)
The class comes together as a whole group. The teacher asks the reporter, photographer and the three focus children to reflect on what they were doing, learning or working on during investigations.

At the end of reflection timethe children will be asked to reset the learning environment for the next part of learning and for investigations the next day. This is planned, careful and calm. They do not necessarily have to pack everything away. Some of their work will be displayed or kept for later in the day or tomorrow.

Formal instruction sessions
After recess, if there are no specialists, you may like to provide a formal instruction session based on the learning intentions listed in the attached sheet.

This can be a whole-group experience but will enable children to work at their own level. If possible, introduce the formal teaching session by using one of the experiences of the children during investigations. This will help to engage the children and link the skill to something meaningful and relevant to the children. It can either be literacy or numeracy or both integrated together.

As much as possible, the WLA does not use cloned art work or worksheets that are the same for each child.

Later in the day
The children may return to their investigations later in the day or you may conduct some reading or writing practice for the children.

The final session
During the last two minutes, it is usual for the children to come together for a final reflection, a game or story together to finish the day.

Play Matters 2nd Edition © Kathy Walker 2011

Parent helper information sheet

Thank you for providing some of your time to our classroom. Your child will enjoy sharing some of their learning with you.

One of the main ways in which the children are learning is through opportunities for them to engage in investigations of interest to them. The teacher will have planned or directed aspects of these investigations with the children and while it may look like they are doing anything they choose, their work is purposeful and linked to literacy and numeracy.

In your time with us there are some key things that you can do to help the children in their learning:

- Read the developmental and learning intentions we have set for all children this fortnight. This will help you to know what types of learning we are concentrating on and you might see opportunities to talk about these things with the children in their investigations.
- Rather than just moving around the room, try to spend time with the same group of children or child for at least 15 minutes.
- The teacher may ask you to help support children in their particular investigations or in the outdoor learning areas.
- Attempt to make links for children with their learning. Instead of asking them, 'What are you making or doing?', try describing some of the things you observe. For example: 'I can see you have placed the round paper on top of the tower', or, 'Would you like to write a list of the things you have used?' This focuses on the learning and concepts of literacy and numeracy rather than just the activity.
- You can make suggestions at times for children who are not sure what to do next, or simply watch and listen to the language of the children.
- The teacher may ask you to talk with a small group about some of their investigations. This is like a small show-and-tell session where the children can model language to each other and share their learning and investigations.

You will notice that the teacher will bring the children back to a reflection time together at some stage during the day in order to help model some learning. Formal instruction time for helping children with spelling, writing or reading also occurs during the day and you may or may not be present for that. The teacher will help you to know what to do at those times. It may be listening to a child read or helping them with their work.

We hope you enjoy your time observing and participating in our classroom and we thank you for your help.

Sample reflection sheet

- Tell us about your investigations today?
- Did you make a plan or do a design brief before you started?
- What were you attempting to do?
- Why are you interested in this?
- Who was working with you?
- What do you plan to work on or do next with this?
- What have you discovered?
- What type of learning did you experience? It seems like you did measuring, writing (whatever was apparent).

Play Matters 2nd Edition © Kathy Walker 2011

References

American Association of School Administrators 1992, *Creating quality schools*, Arlington, Virginia.

Allen, KE & Martos LR, 2007 *Developmental Profiles: Pre-birth through twelve*, 6th edn, Wadsworth Publishing, Belmont, California.

Bornholt, LJ 2005, *ASK-KIDS Inventory for children*, ACER Press, Camberwell, Victoria.

Clarke, P 1992, *English as a 2nd language in early childhood*, 2nd edn, Free Kindergarten Association Multicultural Resource Centre, Richmond, Victoria.

Clarke, P 1999, *Incorporating multicultural perspectives: Planning program for early childhood*, Free Kindergarten Association Multicultural Resource Centre, Richmond, Victoria.

Copple, C & Bredekamp, S (eds) 2009, *Developmentally appropriate practice in early childhood programs: Serving children from birth through age 8*, National Association for the Education of Young Children, Washington DC.

Fisher, JP & Glenister, JM 1992, *The Hundred Pictures Naming Test*, 2nd edn, ACER Press, Camberwell, Victoria.

Gresham, FM & Elliott, SN 2008, *Social skills improvement system*, PsychCorp, Circle Pines.

Hirsh-Pasek, K, Golinkoff, RM, Berk, LE & Singer, DG 2008, *A mandate for playful learning in preschool: Presenting the evidence*, Oxford University Press, New York.

Jones, E & Reynolds, G 1992, *The play's the thing: Teachers' roles in children's play*, Teachers College Press, New York.

Kelly-Byrne, D 1989, *A child's play life: An ethnographic study*, Teachers College Press, New York.

Lindsey, G 1998, 'Brain research and implications for early childhood education', *Childhood Education*, vol. 75, no. 2, pp. 97–100.

Livingston, MJ, McClain, BR & DeSpain, BC 1995, 'Assessing the consistency between teachers' philosophies and educational goals', *Education*, vol. 116, Fall, pp. 124–9.

Marcon, R 2003, 'Reply to Lonigan commentary', *Early Childhood Research and Practice*, vol. 5, no. 1, http://ecrp.uiuc.edu/v5n1/marcon.html

Mares, S, Newman, L & Warren, B 2011, *Clinical Skills in Infant Mental Health*, 2nd edn, ACER Press, Camberwell, Victoria.

Marion, R 2002, *Leadership in education: Organizational theory for the practitioner*, Waveland Press, Long Grove, Illinois.

Mazzuno, R 2001, *Leading to change: Teaching beyond subjects and standards*, John Wiley & Sons, Indianapolis, Indiana.

Miller, E & Almon, J 2009, *Crisis in the Kindergarten: Why children need to play in school*, Alliance for Childhood, College Park, Maryland.

Naylor, S & Keogh, B 1999, 'Constructivism in the classroom: Theory into practice', *Journal of Science Teacher Education*, vol. 10, no. 2, pp. 93–106.

Newberger, JJ 1997, 'New brain development research: A wonderful window of opportunity to build public support for early childhood education!' *Young Children*, vol. 52, no. 4, pp. 4–9.

Privett 1996, 'Without fear of failure: The attributes of an ungraded primary school', *The School Administrator*, vol. 1, no. 53, pp. 6–11.

Slavin, RE 1990, *Cooperative learning: Theory, research and practice*, Prentice Hall, Englewood Cliffs, New Jersey.

Stacey, S 2009, *Emergent curriculum in early childhood settings: From theory to practice*, Redleaf Press, St Paul, Minnesota.

Stone, JG 2001, *Building classroom community: The early childhood teacher's role*, NAEYC, Washington DC.

Strike, K & Posner, G 1985, 'A conceptual change view of learning and understanding', in L West & A Pines (eds), *Cognitive structure and conceptual change*, Academic Press, New York, pp. 211–31.

Summers, L (ed.) 1994, *Quality in teaching and learning: Making it happen*, Edith Cowan University, Perth.

Time, Learning and Afterschool Task Force 2007, *A new day for learning*, Charles Stewart Mott Foundation, Flint, Michigan, http://www.edutopia.org/pdfs/ANewDayforLearning.pdf

Walker, K 2009, *Executive summary: Research findings related to the implementation of the Australian developmental curriculum*, Early Life Foundations, Elwood, Victoria, http://walkerlearning.com.au/info/research-reports-the-australian-developmental-curriculum

Weinstock, HR, Starr, RJ & Fazzaro, CJ, 1974, 'Comparing secondary teachers on logical consistency in educational philosophy and flexibility in teaching', *Instructional Science*, vol. 3, no. 2, pp. 115–126.

Wood, E & Attfield, J 2005, *Play, learning and the early childhood curriculum*, Paul Chapman Publishing, London.

Wright, SP, Horn, SP & Sanders, WL 1997, 'Teacher and classroom context effects on student achievement: Implications for teacher evaluation', *Journal of Personnel Evaluation in Education*, vol. 11, pp. 57–67.

Index

assessment, 10, 35; contrast with testing, 79; diagnostic, 80; strategies, 80–1
associative play, 19, 50, 67

benchmarks & standards, 67, 78–9, 106, 112, 114
boys, 4, 7, 14, 26, 51, 113

child-initiated play, 19
children with disabilities see special needs children
children with English as a second language, 47, 95, 102
classroom organisation, 46–7, 50–1, 52; *see also* learning environment
computer games, 49
computers, 49, 91
constructive play, 18, 70
cooperation, between young children, 8, 67
cooperative play, 19

definition of terms, 9, 11
development of children, 4–5, 6, 8–9, 13, 14, 19–20, 27–8, 68, 72, 78; neurological studies of, 21; record of, 73
developmental domains, 8, 28, 67–8, 70, 71, 112
developmentally appropriate practice, 2, 5–8, 26, 30, 98
directed play, 18
dramatic play, 18, 19, 20, 39, 47, 69, 70, 87, 88, 95, 103, 108, 109, 114
duty of care, 51–2

explorative play, 18
extrinsic rewards, 10, 39

focus children, 13, 28, 29, 57, 58, 59, 61, 68, 72, 81, 98, 100, 102, 107
'freebie', 13, 29, 58, 59, 94, 100

girls, 7, 14, 113

implementation of WLA, 34–42
implementation plan, 36–7
Indigenous children, 101, 102, 103
intentional teaching, 8, 13, 28, 46, 47
intrinsic rewards, 10, 39
investigations, 28, 29, 47, 56, 58, 61, 112–3 *see also* literacy & numeracy; play
investigative play, 8, 18, 20, 86

leadership, school, 12, 34–5, 36, 78, 106, 113
learning centres, 7, 10, 30, 47–50, 48
learning environment, 46–7, 91–2, 94, 102; indoor spaces, 47–51; outdoor spaces, 51–2; special needs children, 100–1
literacy, 87 see also literacy & numeracy
literacy & numeracy, 20, 26, 60, 88–90, 112, 113–4; in WLA, 86; resources for, 52, 90–4

materials, 18, 39, 46–52, 71, 91–4, 95, 109; culturally relevant, 101
mentoring, of teachers, 36–7, 38, 40
misunderstandings, about WLA, 12–13, 113–4

numeracy, 88; resources, 94; see also literacy & numeracy

onlooker play, 19
oral language, 20, 94–5
outdoor spaces, 51–2

parallel play, 19
parent information, 36, 38, 40–1, 81, 106–9, 113–114

pedagogical continuum, 6
peer assessment, by children, 80
personalised learning, 3, 4, 8, 19, 27, 29, 68, 86
philosophy of teaching & learning, 34
photographer (child), 28, 29, 57, 58, 59, 61, 102
planning by teachers, 28; principles of, 66–7; stages of, 67–72
play theorists, 18
play: importance in learning, 5, 9, 18, 20–2 types of, 18; stages of, 19; characteristics of, 19–21
portfolios, children's, 72–4, 80
preschool, WLA in, 30
professional development, 35, 37, 38

record sheet, daily, 57, 72; individual, 72, 73–4
reflection, 28, 58–9
report forms, 80–1
reporter (child), 28, 29, 57, 58, 59, 61, 102
reporting, 81–2
research, on education, 22
resources, see materials
rotations, 60, 86, 102
routine, 69, 113, & special needs children, 99–100

scaffold, defined, 61–2
scrapbooks, 50, 72–3, 91–2
self-assessment, by children, 80
sensory play, 18, 48
social skills, 20, 26, 68

SOI see statement of intent
solitary play, 19
special needs children, 98–9, 100–1
standardised testing, 79
standards see benchmarks & standards
statement of intent (SOI), 68–9, 70, 107
study tours, 37, 38
symbolic play, 19

teacher, role in WLA, 61–2
teacher/parent/student meetings, 81
teaching and learning theory, 3
terminology, 67 see also definitions
tests, see standardised testing
timetable see typical day
topics, 60
'tuning in', 28, 57, 57–58
typical day, 56–62

Walker Learning Approach (WLA): developmental practice, 10; key aspects, 13–14; philosophy, 14; aims of, 26–7; key principles of, 27–8, 108–9; core elements of, 28–9; in preschool, 30; translation into existing practices, 38; misunderstandings about, 12–13, 113–4
whole-school approach, importance of, 34–5
WLA see Walker Learning Approach
worksheets, 20, 39, 80, 94, 108

Engagement Matters

Personalised learning for Grades 3 to 6

Kathy Walker & Shona Bass

Following the success of *Play Matters*, with its action-based focus on learning from preschool to Grade 2, Kathy Walker and Shona Bass have developed the next stage of the Walker Learning Approach for implementation with primary school students in Grades 3 to 6. **Engagement Matters** provides a step-by-step, practical guide for teachers, emphasising student engagement, empowerment and achievement, and importantly, personalised learning. The transition from Grade 2 into the middle and upper primary years is made seamless through the provision of tips, activities and explanatory theory. The book contains a full-colour section of photographs to highlight key themes, and downloadable template documents for planning, assessment and reporting activities.

The processes and tools outlined in this informative and inspiring resource will equip schools with the capacity to actively engage students in their learning across all subject areas and in diverse contexts. In so doing, **Engagement Matters** effectively lays the foundations for ongoing engagement and successful learning throughout school life and beyond.

www.ingramcontent.com/pod-product-compliance
Lightning Source LLC
Chambersburg PA
CBHW061126070526
44584CB00033B/4231